BLADE® PRESENTS

Knives

The World's Greatest Knife Book

2025

EDITED BY
JOE KERTZMAN

Published by

Gun Digest® Books, an imprint of Caribou Media Group, LLC
Gun Digest Media
5583 W. Waterford Ln., Suite D
Appleton WI 54913
gundigest.com

To order books or other products call 920.471.4522 ext. 104
or visit us online at gundigeststore.com

CAUTION: Technical data presented here, particularly technical data on handloading and on firearms adjustment and alteration, inevitably reflects individual experience with particular equipment and components under specific circumstances the reader cannot duplicate exactly. Such data presentations therefore should be used for guidance only and with caution. Caribou Media accepts no responsibility for results obtained using these data.

ISBN: 978-1-959265-29-0

Edited by Joe Kertzman and Corey Graff
Designed by Jong Cadelina
Cover design by Gene Coo

Printed in China

10 9 8 7 6 5 4 3 2 1

I n November 1996, I started a new job as associate editor of *BLADE* Magazine at Krause Publications in Iola, Wisconsin, a three-hour drive north from where my wife, Tricia, and I had been renting the upper flat of a historic farmhouse in Elkhorn. Tricia stayed behind with our dog until she could find work near Iola. We were young. We needed two incomes, and she had a job in the marketing department of another company, Reiman Publications, where we met in the southern suburbs of Milwaukee.

I started my new job, worked a couple of 16-hour days and called her, saying, "Tell my boss I'm coming home, and I want my old job back. This is crazy." Tricia talked me off the cliff, and I stayed with *BLADE* for 19 good years. *BLADE* Editor Steve Shackleford and I put the magazine together every month for nearly two decades. Steve lives outside of Chattanooga, near McDonald and Ooltewah, Tennessee. We worked together via phone, fax and email.

Steve is the rare, impeccable journalist who ensures he gets all his nouns, predicates, apostrophes and dashes in the right places and cares wholeheartedly about the subject matter—knives. He fell in love with the knife industry and advocates for knife journalism integrity, knifemakers and companies, knife rights and ownership.

Shortly after I started with *BLADE*, Steve phoned from Tennessee and asked me to go into the photo archives and find a picture of a handmade knife. He described it and told me to look in the Jim Stone folder. I searched hard, returned to the phone, and said, "Steve, I looked under his first and last names, and I can't find a folder for Jim Stone." In his Tennessean accent, he replied, "No, not Jaem Stone, gemstone."

One day, our magazine designer, Kim Schierl, came into my cubicle laughing. Steve had called her to discuss a page layout. When she answered the phone, Steve said, "Keeim!" She replied, "Hi, Steve." And he blurted out, "How'd you know it was me?"

At one of my earliest BLADE Shows, Spyderco Founder Sal Glesser and his staff invited Steve and me to dinner in Atlanta. Sal took us to a high-end sushi restaurant, and in the late 1990s, there weren't too many around Iola or Ooltewah. Sal put us immediately at ease and played a little game, saying, "I'll order platters of sashimi for everyone, and we'll work our way up from kindergarten to high school, college and then graduate school." The first platter was raw tuna and salmon, which tasted surprisingly good to Steve and me. Then came caviar, eel, squid and even raw shrimp. Steve and I scarfed it down, no problem. We were the only ones to make it to graduate school—raw sea urchin (a Japanese delicacy; I've since heard it's good if prepared properly). However, it must not have been prepared right, or we got a bad piece of urchin. Steve and I took a chunk, looked at each other and bit in. It was the most godawful thing I've ever put in my mouth, texturally and taste-wise. I choked it down and put on my best smile of denial. Steve did the same. Two days later, I was back in the office in Iola when Steve phoned. I answered, and he said, "I can't get that taste out of my mouth!"

A publishing executive in Iola invited Steve to Wisconsin for some brainstorming sessions on improving *BLADE*, increasing circulation and advertising, generating fresh editorial columns and making it a more fascinating read for a wider audience. The night after Steve arrived, we all went out for dinner, including spouses. Chris Williams was the BLADE Show coordinator at the time, and she was telling Steve what a pleasure I was to work with and how I had a positive attitude and was always smiling. Steve, who had gotten used to my youthful overexuberance, said, "Yeah, Joe's a good egg, a little too much cream between his Oreos, but he's alright." I've never seen my wife laugh so hard. Later, she told me she had no idea what he meant, but it seemed to sum me up perfectly.

Steve is a pillar of the knife industry, a friend, and a longtime coworker who I think of often. I haven't talked to Steve in a long time. I think I'll pick up the phone and give him a call. But before I do, I dedicate this book to Steve Shackleford and acknowledge his dedication to the craft and knife industry. Thank you, Steve.

Contents

On The Cover

Standing proudly at far left on the front cover of *KNIVES 2025* is Jerry McClure's exquisite "Straight 8" gent's folder parading a 2 7/8-inch 15N20-and-1084 damascus blade, black lip mother-of-pearl handle scales and Marianne Kelly Art Deco bolster engraving. Matt Parkinson's "Ashokan Moon" small cleaver next to it showcases a pictorial mosaic damascus blade with shapes cut and assembled into a billet that is forge welded together, a silicon bronze bolster and pin, and sculpted Koa wood handle. The red acrylic handle stands out on Kevin Cross's small chef's knife, sporting a 6-inch, flat-ground MagnaCut blade and a pictorial handle pin to complete the package. Next is a Zane Dvorak keyhole integral model done up in the maker's "Ghost Fire" damascus and a handle of black ebony from Ghana. At the bottom right rests a White River Knife & Tool M1 Skinner enlisting a 3-inch CPM S35VN stainless blade with high finger grooves for enhanced control, a full, extended tang, lanyard hole, green G-10 handle, and orange G-10 liners. *(SharpByCoop photos of the handmade knives)*

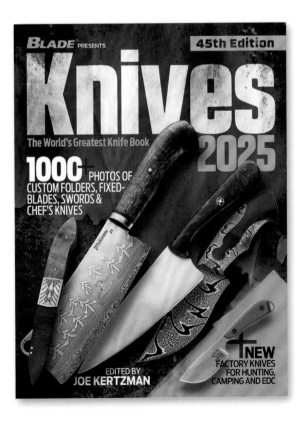

Introduction

"**M**ay I handle?" That quickly became one of my favorite questions at the annual BLADE Show in Atlanta, BLADE Show West, the Badger Knife Show in Janesville, Wisconsin, and the New York Custom Knife Show. The question accomplished so many things at once. It showed that I respected the knifemaker and his work enough to ask to pick it up. By first inquiring whether I could handle a custom knife instead of just grabbing it, the maker knew I had experience at knife shows. I understood that fingerprints, oil on my fingers, and acid from my hands could ruin the finish of highly polished pieces, and it showed that common courtesy and manners are missing in many public places.

The question usually generated a positive response and got my mitts on some incredible knives. Once permission was granted, to open a tricky folder adeptly, press an auto button, or better yet, a frame release, hang on tightly to the handle, maneuver around the edge, unlock the lock, or take a non-threatening and appropriately non-silly stance while holding the edged tool or weapon were all just rewards for the polite inquiry.

I loved handling knives at shows while in my position as managing editor of *BLADE* magazine. I also thoroughly enjoyed the knife shows. The number of tables, booths, demonstrations, presenters, dealers, enthusiasts and collectors at the annual BLADE Show is truly mindboggling and unmatched. There isn't a fine art show that I've been to—and my wife, Tricia, and I enjoy attending those in our area, including the larger ones in metropolitan areas—that comes anywhere close to the BLADE Show for pure extravagance, workmanship, artistic wonder and sheer numbers of exhibitors and attendees. The BLADE Show is something to behold, a showcase of knives.

To put together the other showcase of blades—the *KNIVES* annual—is a labor of love, and one helped along by thousands of quality high-resolution images submitted by photographers for consideration and potential inclusion in the book. Makers pay photographers who spend hundreds of hours setting up lights, finding beautiful backgrounds and taking pictures of shiny blades, detailed embellishments, sculpted features, sharp edges, and even the inner workings of knives. They see the beauty of functional art. The material makeup, artistic renderings, tight fits and finishes, moving parts, metallurgy, machining, forging and handwork result in a one-of-kind craftsmanship that never gets old.

There are always new Trends, State of the Art movements and Factory Trends. The book repeats many categories year after year, but the knives in the tried-and-true sections don't resemble those that came before them. Innovations and advancements abound, and something is always trending in handmade and production knives. "Works in Westinghouse Micarta" are trendy this year, and the continued fusion of synthetic handle materials, including resin, is a hot area. Harpoon blades, "Funereal Coffin Handles," handmade bowies, modern folders, "Native American Weaponry," replicas of international knife and sword designs, "Lordly Swords," hunters, bowies, classic fixed blades, fighters, and "Whetted Foodie Ware" are hot Trends in the *KNIVES 2025* book.

"Folders that Flash," sculpted steel, "Engraved & Enlivened Steel," detailed damascus, carving, "All the Beautiful Burls," "Maestros of Mosaic Damascus," "Pounding out Plumage [feather damascus]," and "Sans Straight Lines" are "State of the Art" sections worthy of more than a little time. Knives with "Meteoric Makeup" get some love, as do those exhibiting "Still Life Scrimshaw" and others "Struck by the San Mai Smiths."

One writer wanted to pen an article on the Japanese Nata knife, saying it defies description, but then he described it beautifully. Another feature focuses on the history of folding knives, "From Penny Knives to Pocket Folders." Knifemaker Kevin Cashen explains "How to Choose the Right Blade Steel," Richard D. White solves some of cutlery's history mysteries, American Bladesmith Society Master Smith Rick Dunkerley touts sole authorship in knifemaking, controlling all aspects of the craft, Wally Hayes describes an amazing week and cast of characters he taught to forge blades at the home of Marina Guinness (yes, those Guinnesses), in Ireland, Les Robertson covers hunting knife design following function, and Ernest Emerson describes "Our Tool, Our Craft, Our Passion, Our Legacy" and an overwhelming love of knives. The book showcases some of the world's most beautiful and functional knives. And the best part is, you don't have to ask, "May I handle?" Just pick it up, flip through the pages, do a little reading and enjoy.

—Joe Kertzman

Wooden Sword AWARD

When Ken Onion was inducted into the *BLADE* Magazine Cutlery Hall of Fame in 2008, he became the 45th and youngest living member to receive the honor. Known for the SpeedSafe assisted-opening mechanism on folding knives, his designs are breathtaking, and his innovation is seemingly endless.

Upon receiving the images on this page from photographer Mitchell Cohen, this year's choice of the Wooden Sword Award winner became obvious.

The first image shows four knives in Ken's Bump series, including his Forum Bump (right), a production prototype, and two Kershaw models. The second image (lower-right) showcases three fixed blades: a stacked-handle drop-point hunter sold by Ken at his first show, a Kershaw Zero Tolerance 0100 prototype, and a modern military utility knife.

The final four folders (below), from top to bottom, are a "Stylus" model with a handle laser engraved in a feather theme by Ken, a second piece laser engraved in a "Facet" bomber motif, an unreleased prototype with a green handle referred to by some as "The Queen's Knife," and at bottom, a prototype one-off flipper folder.

I bestow Ken Onion with the 2025 Wooden Sword Award for his creativity, dedication to the craft, and contributions to the industry and community.

—Joe Kertzman

Forging Blades

FOR MARINA GUINNESS IN IRELAND

Like sipping good Guinness, the overall experience was as heady as the beer.

By Wally Hayes, American Bladesmith Society Master Smith

*I*n 2018, a master watchmaker named Lars Tidemann of Norway, who had been collecting my knives, invited me to visit his friend, Marina Guinness, in Ireland. Marina is part of the Guinness Irish brewing dynasty. Tidemann spoke to Guinness, and they thought it would be great for me to visit her and do a forging demonstration. Guinness graciously provided airfare and lodging.

An amazing week and cast of characters made for the best experience a person could imagine, and I am happy to share this chance-of-a-lifetime, action-packed week with readers. We spent the mornings forging knife blades and the afternoons being shown around Ireland.

The backstory to this adventure, however, started years ago. After Tidemann started collecting my knives, he asked if I could make damascus watch dials. We collaborated on a watch project and crafted many samples as gifts for his friends, including Guinness's son, Finbar. One of the knives Tidemann commissioned me to make was to be a Christmas gift for Guinness. It became the biggest bowie knife I have ever made.

I arrived in Dublin at 10 a.m. and waited for Tidemann to arrive from Oslo, Norway. Guinness came and picked us both up. On the way to her place, we stopped for a tour of a microbrewery owned by her friends and were given a case of mixed beer to go. She asked me if I wanted to drive, but being from Canada, it was the wrong side of the road for me in Ireland, and the vehicle was a semi-automatic that I'd never driven before, so I decided to pass. There are roundabouts, and the roads are roughly a single lane wide.

The long laneway into Guinness's estate is lined with giant, old trees. Once we were settled in the house (I was lost all week), we checked out the forge. She and Finbar had fixed up a large empty stone horse stall into a forging room. It included a steel table with a propane forge, tongs and a side grinder borrowed from the local farrier.

Next, we went into town to purchase safety gloves and glasses and stopped at a local garage to pick up some old leaf springs to forge into blades. I also scrounged steel around the Guinness farm, and we used old broken pitchforks and a hoe.

An art student, Tuqa, was also staying at the house. Tuqa invited her friends from the local arts university to forge during the week. Many living in cottages on the estate also came to the house in the morning for tea. Tommy and his lovely family are included in the cast of characters. Tommy is a local gypsy and musician who helps Guinness and builds gypsy wagons on the estate. His wife helps with house chores, and their boys would pop in and out.

That evening, Tidemann took me out for supper and showed me around Dublin with Tommy, our Uber driver for the week. We stopped and took a picture with a bronze statue of Phil Lynott, a British-born Irish musician and lead vocalist for Thin Lizzy. We jammed with the buskers and, after supper, met a Brazilian boxing champ. Fun times.

The author was invited to the Marina Guinness estate in Ireland to conduct blade-forging demonstrations for her and her guests.

Banging Steel

After tea the next morning, Tidemann, Tuqa, and I went to the forge and began banging steel. I first taught Tuqa how to forge a point out of a round bar from the pitchfork tines I had cut up. We called them zombie spikes. Tuqa took to forging and ended up teaching her friends. I showed her how to twist the zombie spike, forge-taper the ends, and turn it into a circle for holding string. Outside the forge building was a shale pile from old roofs around the estate. I tried some to sharpen our steel implements, and it worked. I added water and demonstrated how the stone removed material to polish or sharpen a tool.

Tidemann decided to forge a bushcraft knife. One of the first people to stop in from the cottages was Glen Hansard and his guitar player, who had just come in from Italy and was heading back out later that day to Paris. Hansard starred in the movie "Once" and is a singer/songwriter and guitar player. He recently played (in November 2023, five years after I visited Ireland) at the funeral of Shane MacGowan, lead lyricist for the Pogues.

Tuqa's friends showed up from the university. They all loved forging pointy things, and a couple were handy with a hammer. All had fun. Tuqa kept an eye on everyone and shared what she learned with them. Tommy was also helpful and showed me the beautiful gypsy wagon he was building from scratch. He asked if I had time to show him how to forge a bracket for his axles. We put our heads together and figured out a plan, and he bought a piece of mild steel to make the brackets. That week, we forged out four

Lars Tidemann (left) of Norway collects knives made by Wally Hayes (right) and arranged for Hayes to visit Guinness and conduct blade forging demonstrations, as seen here.

brackets, and he finished another four on his own. He cut the pieces, and we forged each over a pipe in the vise.

That afternoon, Guinness took Tidemann and I on two stops. First was to meet her friend, acclaimed singer Marianne Faithfull, who was Mick Jagger's girlfriend from 1966 to 1970. She was at a nursing home mending a shoulder. It was nice to meet her and say "Hi." The next stop was to meet Marina's father, Desmond Guinness, who lives in a 450-year-old castle that was so exciting to see. She gave us a tour and spoke about a lot of unique history. The backyard had a pool put in during Roman times and a rose garden wall, which was built to be hollow so gardeners could build fires to keep roses alive in the winter. The castle library was incredible, housing 300-year-old books, some as big as a suitcase. One of the rooms is Jagger's for when he visits.

After forging spikes and bushcraft knives in the morning, we went to Castletown for ice cream.

(Desmond Guinness gave the Castletown estate and property to Ireland.) When Marina Guinness was younger, she and Mick Jagger would ride horses from her dad's castle to Castletown. Inside the high foyer, she gave Mick a dollar to walk around the ledge on the second floor.

Tuqa and I stopped at a local pub for a bowl of Irish stew. Guinness also took me to her friend Charlie's estate for a tour. The house is huge and includes four kitchens from different periods. It even has a haunted room closed for over 100 years. Charlie told me the story of when he rented the house out for a movie, the haunted room was used for a scene, and when they returned the following day, the room was all askew. Charlie said he took the film crew into town for breakfast to settle their nerves so they could continue the video shoot. He showed me the room. The drapes surrounding the bed were sun-faded, and there was a secret closet. One room had an 8-track reel-to-reel Fostex recorder that belonged to Phil Lynott of Thin Lizzy.

Lars Tidemann displays the bushcraft knife he forged during a barbecue at the Marina Guinness estate. The knife is also shown after he finished the handle at home.

Charlie's son, Davie, came over to Guinness's and forged a bushcraft knife and a chisel for his dad. Davie had a lot of great questions. For heat-treating, we used a can of vegetable oil to harden the blades and the kitchen stovetop to temper them and the zombie spikes. We tempered everything to a golden straw color as the stove had no temperature guide. The old gas stoves in Ireland have big, unique burners.

During my stay, the family had a 30-year commemoration of Marina's mom's passing. The commemoration was held at the circa-1720s The Conolly Folly, where her mother is buried. Guinness's friend, Victoria Mary Clarke, who was married to MacGowan until his recent passing, helped prepare for the celebration.

Forging Demo

As guests arrived for the celebration, I went out to do some forging, and they came out for a demonstration. I met Mausi Einsiedel. Her parents live in and own the white castle in Germany that inspired the Disney castle in Florida. Her husband forged a bit, and Marina's brother also showed up to check out the forging activity. Then we all met at the Folly to celebrate.

Tidemann and I helped set up lunch, and Tommy was there with his family. The township opened The

---

Wally Hayes poses in a library in Desmond Guinness's 450-year-old castle that houses 300-year-old books, some as big as suitcases.

Conolly Folly just for us, and at the top of this stone building, you could see across the county. Victoria Mary Clarke interviewed me for her Dublin radio show during this time. We sat in her car looking at The Folly with her tape machine running. I did an hour-long interview explaining my story and promoting the American Bladesmith Society. She asked me many questions about knifemaking, and I am sure it opened some eyes.

A group came back to the house after the family celebration, including Mary Clarke. I brought two pocket folders to Ireland as gifts. They were my Vampire folder fashioned in collaboration with Vknives. Mike Vellekamp, owner of Vknives, lasered initials into the blades for me, one folder with Marina Guinness's initials and the other for Johnny Depp with his initials. Depp—who was coming to work on a movie about Shane MacGowan—was planning to attend on Friday but couldn't make it after his band Hollywood Vampires booked more shows. So, I gave the folder to Mary Clarke for Depp's manager, and we shot a video to send him about the knife. Depp replied right away with his regards, saying, "Tell Wally I'm sending a coin." Cool!

The radio show aired two days later, and we sat around the kitchen table listening to it. Mary Clarke also invited Lars and me to her place to meet MacGowan for a visit and a glass of wine. We took her up on the invitation the next night and went over with Tommy, an incredible musician who has played often with MacGowan over the years. Lars and I made a watch together that he had given Shane

earlier. When we met him, MacGowan wore a watch Tidemann and I previously made for him, which he said he liked a lot. Tommy and MacGowan sang and told stories. MacGowan took a picture with us and signed a book for me that Victoria Mary Clarke wrote.

The next morning, Tommy's son Tom came over, and we reforged a broken bike part of his. When we returned, we all watched a band, which had been in the living room practicing the day before, on TV. which had been in the living room practicing the day before. Guinness said there were boxes of armor in the attic if I wanted to see them, but I never had a chance to investigate further.

Finbar showed me some of his swords and was interested in forging. We fired up the forge and banged on a big chunk of leaf spring. He had fun moving steel. We put a dozen guys

together one day to move a huge wooden table from the house to the greenhouse Finbar was building. Finbar, who has a green thumb, grows hot peppers and raises chickens. Tidemann and I barbecued and shared all my BBQ secrets with Finbar.

Thanks again, Marina Guinness, for your generous hospitality! □

As a guest at the Marina Guinness estate during the forging demonstrations, Davie takes a stance with the bushcraft knife (in his left hand) and zombie spike (in his right hand) he forged.

Wally Hayes was privileged to visit Desmond Guinness's home, a 450-year-old castle.

Wally Hayes poses with Victoria Mary Clarke, who was married to Shane MacGowan of the Pogues until his passing in November 2023.

One of the knives Lars Tidemann commissioned Wally Hayes to make was a Christmas gift for Marina Guinness, shown here holding it. It is the largest bowie knife Hayes has ever made.

How to Choose the Right Blade Steel

Intended cutting use and blade style help determine the ideal alloy for you and your knives.

By Kevin Cashen

Three critical aspects of creating or choosing a quality blade are steel selection, heat treatment and geometry. This feature focuses on the first of these, and the first any aspiring knifemaker or enthusiast will be tasked with—choosing the right blade steel for you and your knives.

To the casual observer, the steel selection process wouldn't seem like such a big deal, but as in-depth as this article is, it barely scratches the surface of the topic.

Not all steels are created equal. Each varies as much as knife style and is designed for a specific application. So, matching the correct steel to the specific blade, intended use, and maker or user can be critical in creating a quality tool. Choosing the best alloy for your purpose can mean the difference between achieving the highest performance by effortlessly allowing the steel to do what it does best and

struggling to pound a square peg into a round hole by forcing it to do something it was never designed to accomplish.

From my observations after a lifetime of providing metallurgical consulting services for various industrial clients and countless knifemakers, the latter rarely select steel with the same analytical vigor as the former. Rather than independent research to match steel chemistry to a process

As far as simple carbon steels go, 1095 is often a favorite for edge holding, just the thing for a fine-cutting kitchen knife like this one by Jeremy Bartlett.

and product, knifemakers often choose whatever alloy everybody else is using.

Be it a ubiquitous old favorite or the newest rage in the "steel of the month club," no single alloy is the best fit for every knife, use or maker. On the other hand, the one area where knifemakers often exceed my

Intended Knife Use

The problem is that we often proceed from the wrong direction. Whatever the reason, many knifemakers have already settled on their steel before determining what knife they will fashion, but how can you make the right choice in a material before you even know its intended use?

A better model for success is letting the primary tasks a knife is meant to perform determine needs and goals. Develop a plan to achieve those goals by designing a hand tool that will perform a specific task or even multiple tasks, keeping in mind that the intended uses of a single knife can be much more varied than people think. With the desired tasks for the edged tool in mind, choose the material based on the desired properties inherent to each steel's specific chemistry. Equally important is

American Bladesmith Society Journeyman Smith John Schultz chose well with 1075 steel for its natural toughness on his recurved chopper.

industrial clients is letting frugality make the choice. The number of knifemakers who have told me they use a specific type of steel because of their access to a cheap or free supply is unfortunate.

The trouble with these approaches is needlessly steepening the learning curve for many a new maker or knife user. I can't count the number of times I have heard a frustrated knifemaker state that an alloy they have tried is a bad steel. But there is no such thing as bad steel. Industry wouldn't bother wasting time, effort or money on steel that wasn't optimum for its intended purpose. There are poor application choices and bad heat treatments. Any fault lies with the knifemakers or bladesmiths and not the steel.

A36 is an excellent steel choice for use in buildings and bridges, but it is a bad reflection on knifemakers if they insist on making a blade with it. The steel properties of A36 are not conducive to knife blades. Alloys like 1095 or O-1 can make good hunting knife blades, but if the steels are heat treated like 5160, they won't measure up in edge performance. I can't tell you how often I've bitten my tongue when shown a blade fashioned from steel with barely enough carbon for adequate strength or an abrasion-resistant edge.

If knifemakers have to deviate from standard heat treatment practices with unorthodox extra steps, it is most likely the result of a steel choice that does not match their application or methods. You can undersoak or over-temper a 1% carbon steel sword or use an alloy better suited for such a blade. You can add several steps to heat-treating richly alloyed steel in your forge or choose a steel that readily responds to that heat source.

recognizing the limits of a maker's abilities to work with a given chemistry.

To explain how to choose the correct steel for you and your knives, the myriad of blade designs is distilled down to two primary categories. The first group—fine-cutting knives—is designed to perform keen slicing or aggressive slashing. They are most often used in a draw-type cut that is optimized like a saw at the microscopic level. Think of scalpels, skinning and hunting knives, and many kitchen knives. Their edges are thin, flat or hollow ground for cutting various soft, fibrous materials.

This group has a subcategory of blades, including some kitchen knives and razors, that will be identical

Rather than using hard and soft layers for damascus, the author, Kevin Cashen, has always combined toughness with abrasion resistance, as in this O1/L6 skinner.

in many design features and desired properties, but they are used more in a push cut. Regardless, impact toughness is not nearly as crucial as abrasion resistance for knives like this.

In contrast, the second group—choppers—is used in straight-on, push-type motions, cleaving, or cutting that often involves impact. These knives cut more like a chisel than a blade drawn into a cut like a saw. Camp knives, some bowies, and many swords fall into this category. They benefit from polished, beefier, convex edge grinds that don't require abrasion resistance as much as impact toughness.

By definition, a knife is a cutting tool. If we should ever find ourselves detracting from a blade's ability to cut in any part of our plan or execution thereof, we may need to consider whether making a knife or another tool is the better option.

Thus, all the properties discussed herein are relevant to cutting. A fundamental condition for a blade to slice through material is that it must be stronger than the cutting medium. There is tremendous load pressure at the microscopic level, where the cut is initiated. So, almost by definition, strength must be a top priority in any knife edge.

For this article, strength is the ability to resist deformation under load. Opposing this prized quality of strength is ductility, or the ability to easily deform without edge or blade failure. Knifemakers heat treat steel to replace ductility with strength. For millennia, it was the job of the blade maker to find the most acceptable compromise between strength and ductility for their blades to cut while avoiding brittle failure.

Steel Strength

There are many types of strength in steel. Examples are compressive strength and tensile strength. These and shear strength are not as apparent in general knife use, so knifemakers more easily conceptualize them as hardness.

The other quality prized in a blade is toughness, which should be viewed as the steel's ability to withstand shock from sudden loads rather than bending in a ductile manner under gradual load. These are two entirely different behaviors, with one being more relevant to a blade used in chopping. Rather than the Faustian bargain of trading strength for ductility, the Holy Grail of blade making is maintaining high strength with impact toughness. In chopping-type blades, impact toughness is almost as valuable as strength.

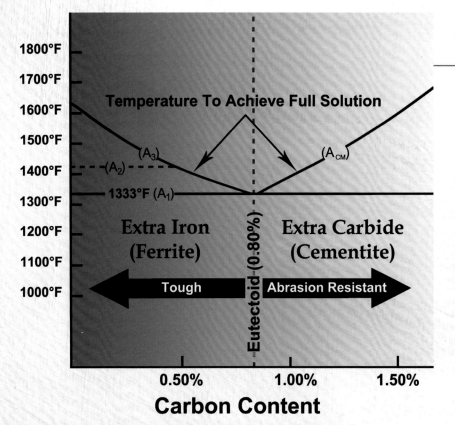

The effects of carbon content in a simple steel can be seen on the Iron-Carbon phase diagram.

which one to use and how to work it. A supplier that provides the chemistry for your steel understands this and is well worth doing business with rather than a source that omits the alloy's makeup.

Carbon content is the first consideration within a steel's chemistry and perhaps the most important. Carbon is the main element responsible for strength in steel. The more carbon a steel has, the greater strength can be achieved in hardening. However, this is only true to a certain point; maximum hardness in carbon steel is achieved at around .80% carbon, and beyond this, not much more is gained in that area. Putting more carbon than .80% into the solution during the hardening process can harm a bladesmith's goals. However, carbon beyond this optimum level will add abrasion resistance if allowed to stay in carbide form.

This sweet spot in carbon levels around .80% is known as the eutectoid. It is the most efficient use of carbon in steel, with no leftover iron (ferrite) or any leftover carbide (cementite). Steels with less than .80% carbon content are inherently tougher and less brittle, while steels with more can have much greater abrasion resistance with a tendency to be less tough. This is important to consider when choosing steel for your intended blade purpose. Does a machete need abrasion resistance? Does a skinning knife need to be tough? Choosing 1075 for one or 1095 for the other could make all the difference in having a steel that will work for you or against you in creating that blade.

In centuries past, bladesmiths had no choice but to compromise between strength and ductility when working with simple iron-carbon material. But then, starting in the early 19th century, alloying changed everything. Finally, with the intentional addition of other elements to steel, bladesmiths could have their cake and eat it, too.

The next property to consider in a knife blade is abrasion resistance. Microscopically, the knife edge is subjected to tremendous wear, even when cutting seemingly soft materials. It is this wear that results in the tool dulling when used. Abrasion resistance is the steel's ability to withstand such friction effects. While this property does increase with overall hardness, steel's unique makeup gives it abrasion resistance above and beyond hardness and even independently from it. Within the steel, there might also be carbide particles with a hardness that far exceeds the overall Rockwell measurement numbers of the blade. Fine cutting and slicing blades benefit more from abrasion resistance than impact toughness.

Although the possible steel choices for modern knifemakers are endless, for simplicity's sake, this discussion is limited to non-stainless alloys commonly used by forgers and grinders alike. Although many knifemakers have become dependent on AISI (American Iron and Steel Institute) or SAE (Society of Automotive Engineers) steel names, such titles as 1084, W-2 or 80CrV2 lack specificity and meaning compared to studying the individual steel's chemistry in determining its potential properties.

I strongly encourage knifemakers to study the chemistry of any potential steel choices to decide

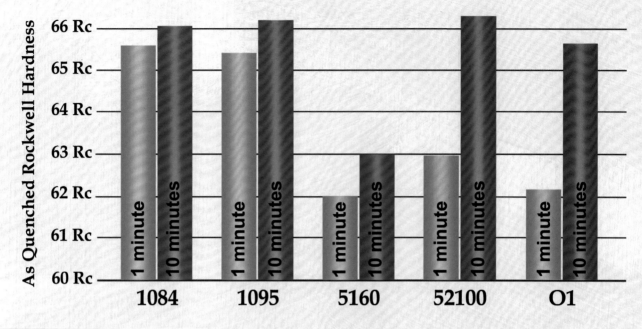

The graph shows the total hardness from proper solution in steels soaked for 1 minute and 10 minutes, respectively, illustrating the effects alloying can have on heating requirements.

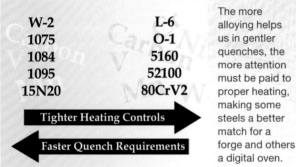

The more alloying helps us in gentler quenches, the more attention must be paid to proper heating, making some steels a better match for a forge and others a digital oven.

Steel Alloys

A sword in the 13th century that had to be kept in the low hardness ranges could now be just as tough at much higher hardness levels. Fine slicing cutters could have an abrasion-resistant carbide boost far exceeding simple cementite abilities. But with these gains in performance came greater demands for more precise controls in heat treating, atmosphere, and more refined blade quenches. Today, even the most basic carbon steels have enough alloys to radically differentiate them from the old steel. Anybody who thought they would water quench 1084, just like traditional tamahagane steel, can attest to this fact.

For this reason, another critical factor must be considered in proper steel selection beyond the type of knife being made. It is why the premise of this article is choosing the right steel for *you* and your knife. Our modern steel alchemists may have created the perfect high-tech steel for a knifemaker's applica-

tion. But if they're learning the ropes, or all they own is a humble forge, it could still be a terrible choice for their knife.

If your shop is equipped with a digitally controlled oven, all the many modern alloy options are available if you learn the rules each steel choice requires. The same chemistry that makes one steel harden in almost any oil or air makes it much more finicky when heated before being quenched. An alloy steel may have the potential to outperform a simple carbon steel, but not if you lack the equipment necessary to unlock that potential.

Figure 1 shows the as-quenched hardness results of a series of tests involving simple heating versus a standard 10-minute soak on commonly used steels. Here, the effect of increased alloying is plain to see when looking at each steel's time and temperature requirements, which many open-flame heat sources or forges may struggle to meet. Unless armed with an excellent understanding of the metallurgy, a smith desiring to stick with more traditional tools would be better served by more traditional steels. Simple carbon steels such as "W" or 10XX series are like what forges were initially made for and will allow the traditional smith to produce a fine blade effortlessly.

Knowing what each of the additional alloying elements brings to the table is valuable in knowing what to seek in steel. If you're looking for impact

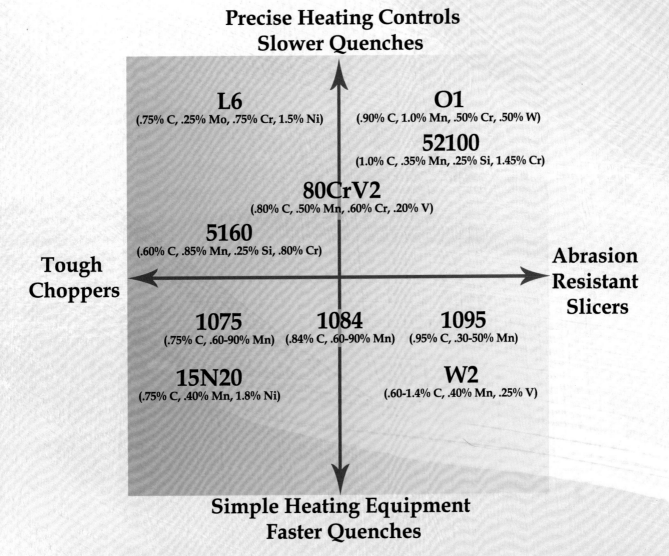

Precise Heating Controls
Slower Quenches

L6
(.75% C, .25% Mo, .75% Cr, 1.5% Ni)

O1
(.90% C, 1.0% Mn, .50% Cr, .50% W)

52100
(1.0% C, .35% Mn, .25% Si, 1.45% Cr)

80CrV2
(.80% C, .50% Mn, .60% Cr, .20% V)

5160
(.60% C, .85% Mn, .25% Si, .80% Cr)

Tough
Choppers

Abrasion
Resistant
Slicers

1075
(.75% C, .60-90% Mn)

1084
(.84% C, .60-90% Mn)

1095
(.95% C, .30-50% Mn)

15N20
(.75% C, .40% Mn, 1.8% Ni)

W2
(.60-1.4% C, .40% Mn, .25% V)

Simple Heating Equipment
Faster Quenches

toughness, consider chemistries that include nickel or silicon. These additions affect the iron's atomic lattice, which acts like a shock absorber. For a knife needing abrasion resistance, a boost from the more powerful carbide formers can give you longer wear than simple cementite, with two of the most common examples being vanadium (above .25% of overall elements) or tungsten. Chromium will also help in this area to a lesser extent.

If you wish to achieve a fully hardened blade with minimal effort, manganese over 1% or relatively modest additions of chromium are just the ticket for leaving behind your stressful days of the water quench. And, of course, for applications where simple carbon steels would rust too quickly, chromium over 11% will also help resist corrosion.

Combining it in one chart helps select the correct steel based on knife use and a knifemaker's heat-treating equipment.

The chart in Figure 2 brings together all these considerations. On a final note, it must be conceded that a skilled bladesmith with a solid knowledge of heat treatment could push several of these alloys into adjacent categories. Still, here, we've focused on the path of least resistance.

By capitalizing on the characteristics of an alloy's chemistry, a maker can spend less time getting it to behave in the desired manner and more time maximizing its performance. □

The lineup includes, from top to bottom, the Kakuri C-14, C-7, C-8, and C-5 models, an antique nata the author purchased on eBay, and a semi-custom Toyokuni Tozan Nata.

The Japanese Nata Defies Description

It's "nata" hatchet, "nata" machete, and "nata" bolo—it's a nata!

By Rod Halvorsen

For decades, my fascination with utility chopping tools suitable for woods carry, hunting chores, and ranch work has exposed me to an endless array of configurations. The more I encounter and use, the more models appear.

Most such blades can be placed into a few categories: machetes, hand axes, hatchets, or bolos and parangs. Some time ago, I was introduced to another edged tool category. You might say it is a species all its own, yet it's "nata" machete, "nata" hatchet and certainly "nata" bolo! What is it? It's a nata! Various English terms can be used to describe the Japanese nata, but none of them alone suffice. Manufacturers use some of those descriptions, yet the proper descriptor doesn't seem to exist in English.

The tasks accomplished efficiently with nata blades fall into the purview of all the groups cited above. While the nata isn't really a hatchet, it chops admirably. Though not a bush knife like a machete, bolo or parang, it clears trails, and absent of being a cleaver, it cleaves.

Nata origins are befogged by time and, for me, the Japanese language. Still, I am informed that the choppers have been popular in Japan with gardeners, woodworkers, loggers and foresters, campers, orchard arborists, and farmers. The nata is a ubiquitous tool among Japanese outdoor enthusiasts.

I contacted two edged-tool manufacturers that supplied me with new nata samples for testing and review. Each company has been making natas for many decades. Within the general nata family, some blades accomplish specific tasks more readily than others, but all share commonalities. Holding a nata for the first time, one immediately feels the stoutness and what might

Two excellent examples of Japanese natas work well when using soft batons (not hardened mauls) against their blade spines to aid in splitting kindling.

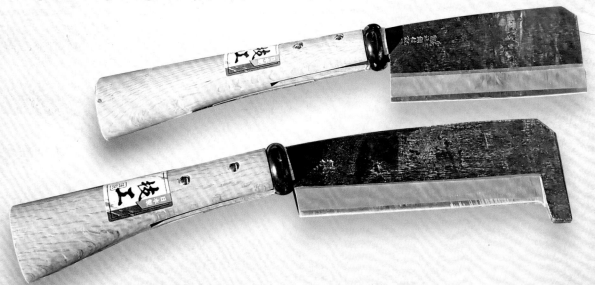

be called a "superabundance of blade." With minimal blade taper and starting at around 1/4-inch thick, the nata blade feels unlike anything else in a handheld chopper. With blade lengths never exceeding 8 or 9 inches, unlike many other choppers like the bolo or machete, they are not long bush knives, hatchets, cleavers, or billhooks. A nata is in a class of its own.

The short blade can deceive one into thinking the nata is a specialty tool for close-up work. Conversely, it is a traditional general-purpose tool. After spending time in the field cutting brush, splitting kindling, butchering elk, cutting meat and chopping vegetables in the kitchen, I'm convinced that the design is one of the most efficient all-around choppers I've ever used. Inch-for-inch and pound-for-pound, the nata serves as well as other edged tools with longer blades.

Single-Bevel Field Knives

A longtime fan of chisel-ground, AKA single-bevel field knives, the edges on several nata models offer the same advantages as my favorite blades. Most nata edges include deep fullers on the unground sides of the blades, and all noticeably arch downward, like steep drop points, from the blade spines to cleaver-like tips.

I'm not entirely sure why the single-bevel blade is not more common on mass-produced bush knives, except that such a grind is best suited to right- or left-handed use. Thus, companies may shy away from offering a product that is limited in its market value, and two versions of each model must be made, one for righties and one for Southpaws like me. This possible limitation does not faze the Japanese makers.

While the most common standard models are made with classic right-hand edges, I was delighted to discover that left-hand options exist and obtained one. Over the years, I've learned to use right-hand chisel-ground edges efficiently. Weak-handed use can be mastered.

All new nata blades I tested came shaving sharp from the factory, and the single-bevel samples possess fine edges. From a Western perspective, such edges might be considered too fine, as they are more fragile than the blades on most machetes or bush knives. As a hobby forger and heavy user of field and bush knives, I have never understood the concept of a blocky reinforced edge. Nor do I agree with the criticism of a heavy-bladed knife having "too fine an edge for field work." I've never encountered a bush knife with an edge that is too fine for fieldwork. I prefer field knives with keen and finely ground edges. It's how I make them myself, and as such, I found all the nata models I obtained to meet that personal preference.

Not surprisingly, with Japanese origins, the blades on the new production nata models I obtained are laminated. Even the antique model

Of superb craftsmanship, the Toyokuni nata isn't just pretty. It's a stout and sturdy working tool.

I purchased on eBay appears to have a forged, laminated blade with a soft spine and hard, high-carbon steel edge. Just as predictably, the laminated blades proved efficient in field use. It's easy to forget, though, how a soft blade spine reacts to a baton, and when the baton happens to be a maul or hammer, peening of the spine is inevitable. In other words, don't use a hardened baton on a nata. In examining several old and worn examples, I noticed the peened spines immediately, so I did not baton new models in the field.

Slicing steaks off an elk quarter was easy using the Kakuri C-5.

I am not sure why the spine peening crops up on old Japanese natas unless such tools were used by carpenters who grabbed what was closest at hand, a hammer, to get the job done.

The multi-use potential of the nata begins with its handle. While the nata blade is short, the handle is long. Choking up on the handle, a short blade allows for fine control. One can imagine its usefulness among carpenters, especially those involved in traditional types of construction like log homes, post-and-beam and timber framing. With an extra inch or two of grip over what a typical machete might offer, slipping the hand down to the wide end of the handle transforms the nata into an effective trail clearer or kindling splitter. Since only a limited section of the edge is used in chopping wood and brush, shifting the hand down can convert a 7-inch field knife into a 13-inch bolo. It works.

Oak Handles

A traditional oak handle is most common across the nata manufacturing spectrum, and it's difficult to think of a better choice. Handle shape combines the narrowness of the upper grip near the blade with a significant swell toward the butt, the former allowing for fine control and the latter ensuring a secure grip for safe handling when chopping. This contrasts with straight-handle bush knives that tend to slip in wet hands when cutting brush, chopping firewood, or field butchering. With a smooth handle finish, the tendency might be to add texturing for better purchase,

though I did not have any problems with the knives as they came from the factory.

The solid oak handles are grooved or mortised to receive 2.75–3.5-inch tangs and then secured with thick collars or ferrules at the ricassos. One or two pins or rivets are pounded through the wood and tangs. Except for the semi-custom Toyokuni model I acquired, where the gap between the wood and tang is skillfully filled and smoothed, no attempt was made on the other models to provide a perfect fit along the top and bottom edges of most tangs. This leaves a gap, which I thought might cause an uncomfortable grip, but that didn't prove to be the case. Choking up and grasping each handle near the tang area was not a problem. Further, when each tool was used for heavy chopping with a lot of friction, my hand was positioned at the swelled base of the grip, where the oak was solid and smooth. The design is an interesting nod to purpose, not pretty.

With the generalities and just a few details put behind us, delving into the specific models tested seems appropriate.

According to the Kakuri Corporation, the four company natas I tested are forge-laminated from SK steel and soft iron. The 18.5-ounce Model C5 with an 8.5-inch, single-bevel blade and the 21.5-ounce, 7-inch, double-bevel C14 Model, both sporting 6.75-inch handles, are close siblings. The blades are each

The Hashi-Tsuki with a tip guard can be used to chop on a hard surface without fear of damaging the edge.

.250-inch thick nearest the handles, with moderate tapers toward the butts. With the overall patterns being almost identical, the two lean toward the parang end of the nata spectrum. Both possess virtually identical handling characteristics separated by about 1.5 (almost unnoticed) inches of blade length and, of course, the impossible-to-ignore difference in edge grinds (single versus double bevel). As such, each excels at performing different chores.

The Model C5 is the star at limbing tree branches without cutting the trunk and making very fine slices on wholesale cuts of meat and vegetables, while the C14 is what you would expect—an all-around bushwhacker and chopper for the field and camp. Both come supplied with wooden scabbards, synthetic frogs suitable for retention of the blades in the scabbards but not appearing designed or strong enough for daily carry on a belt, and synthetic edge guards.

Wide and forward balancing, the Kakuri models are best described as being more hatchet than parang. The 26-ounce Model C7, including a 7-inch, .30-inch-thick, single-bevel blade and a 6.5-inch handle, stands out for its unique tip protuberance that the Japanese call a "Hashi-Tsuki." This is a truly classic type of nata. Described as a protuberance, tip guard or edge guard, steel extends from the down-

ward slope of the blade spine past and beneath the edge at the blade's tip. It serves an admirable purpose—protecting the cutting edge from damage when chopping sticks or carrots on hard surfaces like stone or concrete slabs.

Concrete and Stone

I purposely used the knife to chop cutting media on stone and concrete and later wondered why such a design isn't widely used. It's a great idea! An ancillary purpose for the protuberance of iron is to grab wood or other material being chopped toward the nata user, and despite its ungainly appearance, it proved handy.

Sans edge protector and weighing in at 30 ounces, the Model C8 Kakuri blade is .35-inch thick and the closest to a hand axe or hatchet of all models tested. The most forward heavy of all, it serves the same purposes as any other hand axe—the felling and bucking of small trees, heavy cleaver work on main meat cuts and firewood splitting. It especially excelled at splitting firewood even though the C8 lacks the thickness of most Western hatchets. Laid flat, it would also make a decent tent peg pounder. Indeed, the 8.5-inch handle provides the leverage to accomplish such tasks.

While the Kakuri offerings are fine utilitarian implements best described as excellent additions to garden, camp and hunting equipment, the semi-custom Toyokuni Tozan nata-0031-2, with a .20-inch-thick blade and weighing 13.4 ounces, is in a class of its own, a high class! This is a top-grade hunting knife-style nata. Forged from Hitachi White 2 & Blue 2 steels, the high-carbon and soft iron laminate, as with the Kakuri models, is serviceable and easily sharpened.

Exhibiting truly superb craftsmanship, this nata is about the same overall size as the classic Navy Mark 2 utility knife, though with a blade about an inch shorter. Generalizations aside, it is an entirely different tool. Mine came with a left-hand, single-bevel edge and has become a favored companion in the woods. Small, easy to carry on the belt and disappearing in a rucksack, this chopper lops with effectiveness far exceeding the capabilities one might associate with such a small knife. Inherent to the nata design, the heavy blade and longer-than-usual handle make it all possible. The Toyokuni Tozan was delivered with a wood scabbard of equal quality to the blade it houses. A thick wood block on the scabbard retains a high-quality leather frog for belt carry.

Finally, I obtained an old hard-worn nata from a company that sells used Japanese garden and forestry tools on eBay. I call this one an antique because it looks long in the tooth. With all the standard features of a nata, it appears to have been forged by a local blacksmith of bygone days. With a .25-inch-thick, 7-inch blade, this one weighs in at 1 pound and shows some evidence of a baton being used on the spine. It is designed with the most abrupt spine-to-tip blade drop of all models tested and features a right-hand, single-bevel blade grind. While it looks to have had a hard life, it deserves further attention and a good scabbard. There is a lot of useful service life left in this tool.

It's not often that I find unique chopping blade designs I have no prior experience owning and using. However, the nata is one such type. Whether the end use is in the camp, woods, kitchen or woodshop, the nata has much going for it. Now that I've gained experience with natas, will I ignore them in the future? "Nata" chance! □

Top to Bottom:
For limbing, the single-bevel edge draws the blade away from the cut branch and not into the tree trunk.

The nata handle attachment is unique and serviceable.

The nata models came with scabbards and edge guards.

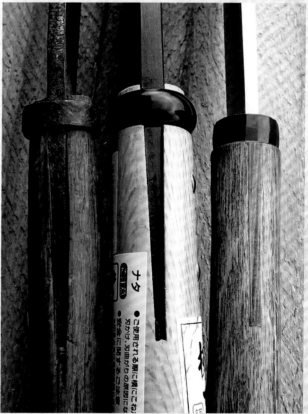

Natas sourced from:

Kakuri Corporation, 3-3 Higashihonjoji, Sanjo City, Niigata Pref., 955-0823 Japan. At writing, available on Amazon.

Toyokuni, Ltd, 783-0071, 728-2 Kameiwa, Nankoku City, Kochi Prefecture, toyokunijapan.com/.

Seller Search Ebay: minorhaned0_fish_n_gamera
For used Japanese woodworking and forestry, garden and camping tools.

Solving Cutlery's
History Mysteries

The company name stamped on the blade isn't always the manufacturer's name.

By Richard D. White

Who doesn't like solving a good mystery? Remember the mystery game Clue, with its colorful game board depicting an old mansion, a stack of character cards, various miniature weapons, a detective's notebook, a set of dice, and clue cards? The object of the game is to determine who murdered the victim, where the crime took place, and which weapon was used. Each player assumes the role of one of six suspects and attempts to solve the whodunnit by strategically moving around the game board that represents rooms of the mansion and collecting clues about the circumstances of the murder from other players. Clue is cited in several Top 10 lists as the fifth highest-selling board game of all time, with over 200 million copies sold.

Mysteries regarding knife production abound because thousands of cutlery manufacturers exist in the United States. Collecting vintage or antique knives inevitably turns up many examples with mysterious or unknown tang stamps and origins, even for seasoned collectors. To many knife enthusiasts, determining which factories produced specific models is unimportant. However, for serious and curious collectors interested in researching some recent finds, tracking down the origins of unknown tang stamps is akin to solving a cutlery history mystery.

In most cases, the finders of these unknown specimens can reference highly regarded publications with lists of knife manufacturers, descriptions of tang stamps, production dates, countries of origin, and sometimes even desirability ratings or collectible rankings.

Such books include those authored by John Goins and Bernard Levine. I use the references much like a history book since they are devoted explicitly to production knife history, perusing years, dates, details and fascinatingly unique information. Of course, there is also the Internet and its various search engines, which, if used correctly, can uncover published data on most little-known knife tang stamps. Keep in mind, however, that much of the Internet, especially forums, consists of a series of posts made by individuals, some experts, but many not. Most posts are simply an individual's opinion and are not based on factual material such as military contracts or production knife company catalogs and ephemera.

Like detective work, looking for clues is the key to solving most knife mysteries. Many knives can reveal clues to their history if one knows where to research and what to look for. Unfortunately, just when you think you've traced a particular knife back to its manufacturing origins, you inevitably discover that thousands of models were not even manufactured by the company indicated on the tang stamp, but were, in fact, made on contract by different factories. Those

The four fixed-blade hunting knives exhibit identical blade shapes, fiber spacer patterns, aluminum pommels, and stacked-leather handle construction, but each has a different blade tang stamp. From left to right, the blades are stamped "Jean Case," "Belnap," "Kinfolks," and "Hollinger."

The same company made two original sheaths of widely different patterns. A page from Dean Case's *Kinfolks Knives* book shows the exact carved leather sheath and proves that the company made it.

factories derived a significant portion of their business taking orders. In other words, the stamping on the blade, which generally indicates a manufacturer and city of origin, may not be the factory or the city where the knife was made.

Production knife companies can be divided into two categories. The first manufactures blades bearing their own stampings and makes few, if any, knives for other businesses. Remington Cutlery appears to be one of those manufacturers that produces only knives bearing the company's full name. Remington did have a couple of production lines, one with knives stamped in a straight-line "Remington," but it only produced its own blades and did not work with outside contracts.

The second are those that not only produced knives bearing the official company name but also accepted contracts to make models for any of several major retail outlets needing factory-fixed blades and folders. For many manufacturers in the second category, making knives for retailers or putting other companies' brand names on tang stamps equated to a significant source of revenue.

Knives on Contract

Some production knife companies made blades on contract to spread their knives throughout the United States. This was particularly important for manufacturers like the Western States Cutlery of Boulder, Colorado, which had difficulty selling its knives east of the Great Plains. Other companies include indus-

try giants like Camillus, Colonial, Western Cutlery and Kinfolks. Some outlets contracting with Western Cutlery to make knives for them included Sears, Montgomery Wards, Coast Hardware, Western Auto, Spiegel and Shapleigh Hardware.

Camillus is perhaps the best example of a production knife company known for copyrighting dozens of tang stamps, yet the manufacturer made all the blades. The list of those stampings takes up pages but includes Kingston, Clover, Sta-Sharp, Dunlap, Kwik-Kut, Streamline, OVB (Our Very Best), High Carbon Steel, Keen Kutter, Kent, Sword Brand, Tip Top and Buck. While most stampings are contract-made knives (like Keen Kutter and Buck), others are merely Camillus Cutlery's sub-brands.

With the data well documented regarding the practice of knife manufacturers producing contract brands, a look at specific examples is in order. The origins of many of the tang stamps started as mysteries that were eventually solved through clues inherent to the knives.

Western Cutlery knives hold some specific clues, which, once recognized, can prove beyond a shadow of a doubt that they were made by the company even when stamped with another name. The first and most obvious clue lies in the aluminum pommels that Western used on its various hunting knives. Unlike the rounded, mushroom-shaped or ovoid pommels of other knife manufacturers, Western employed a bird's-beak pommel.

The aluminum pommel extends smoothly from the

A gorgeous, red-handled hunting knife is stamped "Ideal" on the knife and sheath—the snaps on the top of the sheath hint at its origin.

last series of colorful handle spacers to form a bird's beak and head. The top of the pommel is not flat, as most others, but slanted like a bird's head, sloping down at an angle toward its back. Recognizing this obvious clue, it becomes easy to put a hunting knife stamped "Western" next to those stamped "Craftsman," "Western Field," and "Hawthorne" and recognize that Western Cutlery made them all, and those featuring alternative tang stamps were built under contract for Sears and Montgomery Ward.

A second clue to whether Western Cutlery manufactured specific knives is those stamped with a unique patent number, 1,967,479. The number refers to a patent by Harlow Platts described as a "novel and simple method of forming a handle for a tool which is durable, strong and which cannot be displaced or loosened." The patent refers to Western's double-tang handle configuration, which is two flattened steel rods that run from the blade to the pommel and between which fiber and leather spacers are stacked to form a handle that does not move.

Since only Western knives incorporated the patented handle design, it becomes a simple matter to look at a typical hunting knife from that era to see whether the steel tangs are visible on both sides of the handle, with the spacers lying between the two—Western most certainly made knives with this design feature.

Round Leather Spacers

Most other hunting knife handles from the time were made with a single round rod extending from the base of the blade to the pommel. Round leather handle spacers with holes in the middle are stacked tightly, with the rod running through them, for the length of the handle between the blade and pommel. Generally, the rod is threaded so that a round, usually brass nut can be tightened to sandwich and secure the handle spacers between the blade and pommel, making a durable handle. On these knives, the top ends of the aluminum pommels have round indentations where threaded nuts are seated. Marble's knives are examples of this handle construction.

Over several months, I accumulated four hunting knives with a wide-blade style known as a "woodcraft" pattern popularized by the Marble Arms

A closeup of a Kinfolks yellow-handle knife-axe combination set shows the snap-button sheath attachment style. The second image also shows a red-handle Ideal hunting knife, which snaps onto the Kinfolks hatchet set sheath. Notice the similarities of the leather sheath embossing style—a perfect match. Kinfolks made the "Ideal" knife.

A gorgeous, stag-handled hunting knife stamped "WARD" includes a sheath with unique leather embossing. A closeup of the stag-handle hunter shows the WARD tang stamp and a patent number below it, giving an obvious hint as to the knife's maker.

Company. The knives had four different tang stamps, one reading JEAN CASE CUT. CO., a second, BELNAP, LOUISVILLE, the third, HOLLINGER, and the fourth was stamped KINFOLKS, INC. I was already familiar with the Kinfolks stamp, as I have always favored this wide-blade style. I also knew Kinfolks had a knife factory built in the 1930s but did not realize that the manufacturer was potentially involved in contracts with other companies to produce their knives.

An examination of the four hunting knives laid side by side clearly showed that they were almost identical in blade length, had the same highly polished chrome-vanadium blades, and identical aluminum guards and pommels with brass centering nuts.

If I needed yet another piece of evidence to prove that Kinfolks made the four knives, the spacer pattern proved a strong clue. The knives had identical stacked leather handles ending near the guards with alternating black and white spacers—five black spacers separated by three white spacers. Finally, looking at the sheaths was the icing on the cake. Although all four hunting knives had sheaths of the same length and width, with identical rivet spacing, one was patterned differently from previously known Kinfolks examples. Wondering if this last leather sheath with a unique stamping was original to the knife and produced by Kinfolks, I turned to a book by Dean Elliot Case titled *Kinfolks Knives, a History of Cutlery and Cousins.*

Western was a significant producer of contract knives for Sears, Montgomery Ward, Western Auto and others. Here are four examples branded "The Coast Cutlery," "Western Auto," "Hunt Master" (Spiegel), and "Western Boulder." Some enthusiasts specialize in collecting Western's contract-branded knives.

Looking at the illustrations of various Kinfolks knives in the book, I came across a picture of a sheath identical to that which housed the Jean Case woodcraft knife. The mystery was solved, and all four hunting knives were made by Kinfolks, even though they had different stampings.

A unique hunting knife appeared recently in an Internet auction. Being attracted to colored hunting knife handles from days gone by, I bid on it. My winning bid soon arrived, and opening the package revealed a hunting knife and a leather sheath with the word "Ideal" embossed in script lettering. The blade tang was also etched "Ideal." The mystery was in what production knife company made it. I noticed that, at the top of the leather sheath, were two snaps, one on each side of the pommel. Those snaps led me to rustle through my collection of hunting knives, explicitly looking for knife/axe combination sets. I found just the set, made by Kinfolks, with the same two snaps on the knife sheath and an identical set on the hatchet sheath. Taking the newly purchased Ideal

hunting knife, I aligned the snaps on that sheath to the Kinfolks knife/axe combination set. "Snap, snap," a perfect match.

Examining the leather embossing on the Ideal hunting knife sheath proved to be a perfect match to the Kinfolks sheath for the knife/axe combination set. My investigation solved which company made the Ideal hunting knife with red handle slabs. It was a part of a Kinfolks hunting knife set with an Ideal stamping. I am sure a matching hatchet with an Ideal stamp and a red handle is somewhere.

Different Handle Material

One of Western's most interesting knife styles was a wide-bladed pattern with a different handle material from what it usually used. Western Cutlery was generally known for its stacked-leather knife handles. The H-shaped leather washers are stacked together with various patterns of fiber spacers along the company's patented double-tang handle, all held in place by an aluminum pommel that is double-pinned to two steel tang sections.

The knives I acquired are stamped "West-Cut," indicating Western's less expensive line of knives, most of which incorporate stacked-leather handles. Each of these knives, however, enlists a thin aluminum guard and a shiny, molded handle, which narrows at the butt to form a quasi-shaped pommel. The handles are plastic, deep brown with specks and swirls of lighter browns.

Finding several other examples, which I assumed to be West-Cut's as well, I was struck by the stamping on the blades, which included Shapleigh's, Colonial, Providence, Viking, New York, and yet another with an arched line reading "The Coast Cutlery, Portland, Oregon." The Viking example had an aluminum handle. The Colonial was bright orange, and the Coast Cutlery (not pictured) model featured a relatively thick aluminum guard with a red spacer between two aluminum pieces.

Once again, the mystery lies in which productive factory made the hunting knives. Colonial Cutlery of Providence, RI, was known for making thousands of knife styles with colored handle materials. Living in Colorado, I have located a half-dozen examples of these molded, brown-handled knives.

Also, I know that Coast Cutlery of Portland, OR, had extensive contracts with Western for producing small red and white bird-and-trout knives, reinforcing Western's status as the maker of the molded-handle knives. The "Shapleigh's St. Louis" example is a monkey wrench in the works, as is the "Viking, New York." Both are located quite far from Boulder, and Western Cutlery generally had few contracts to make knives east of the Mississippi River. Colonial Cutlery in Providence is even farther away.

Since Western has been out of business since 1992, and all company records are available to collectors and researchers, the idea that Western produced all these knives is up in the air. A letter to current Providence Cutlery owners was also a dead end. Who made these colored, molded-handle knives? That's a mystery yet to be solved.

Solving cutlery's history mysteries involves following the clues, comparing examples, looking at knife construction, examining the sheaths, reading company histories, talking to other collectors, and formulating educated guesses. □

Two hunting knives, one with a stag handle and the other featuring a sectioned "cracked ice" celluloid handle, have similar "bird's beak" pommels, blade shapes and tang stampings. A closeup comparison of the two hunting knives shows the same patent number on both blade tangs. This patent number was awarded to Western Cutlery for "a simple method of forming a handle for the tool"—the double steel tang upon which H-shaped fiber spacers and washers could be stacked to form the handle. Western made the WARD hunting knife; thus, another mystery was solved.

Hunting Knives:
Design Follows Function

Forethought into the intended use of hunters pays dividends in the forest, wetlands and fields.

By Les Robertson

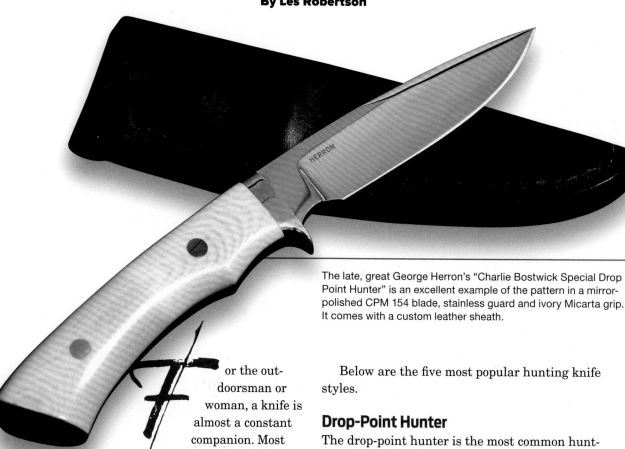

The late, great George Herron's "Charlie Bostwick Special Drop Point Hunter" is an excellent example of the pattern in a mirror-polished CPM 154 blade, stainless guard and ivory Micarta grip. It comes with a custom leather sheath.

For the outdoorsman or woman, a knife is almost a constant companion. Most will carry a knife that falls into the category of a hunter. The *Merriam-Webster Dictionary* defines a hunting knife as a large, stout knife used to skin and process game. Millions of hunting and utility knives have been made over the centuries. Having been a judge for custom knife awards in both the United States and Canada, I can tell you there are some unusual ideas on what is and is not a knife that would fit into the hunter category.

Below are the five most popular hunting knife styles.

Drop-Point Hunter

The drop-point hunter is the most common hunting knife. The drop-point pattern maintains its steel thickness along the spine, and then the blade design gently slopes, or drops, toward the point. Generally, the blade remains slightly thicker at its point than other hunting knife styles. The blade thickness provides the drop-point hunting knife with versatility to not only skin but also disjoint game and pry (though it's not a prybar). These advantages can be significant to the hunter when dressing larger game.

A 6-inch feather damascus blade, damascus guard and mammoth ivory handle define Wess Barnhill's custom hunter with a custom leather sheath. (SharpByCoop photo)

Skinner

The idea of a skinning knife is to remove the skin/fur from the game. Hunters can also use the upswept blade style to dress out game. However, the sweeping shape features a slightly thinner blade and edge for a specific purpose. It is designed for elongated cuts and better blade control, ensuring the fur maintains its integrity.

Semi-Skinner

The semi-skinner blade is the middle ground between the drop-point and the skinner blade. The slightly raised spine hump extends the curved part of the blade for skinning, at the same time maintaining the drop point to avoid puncturing the abdominal cavity. Doing so could taint the meat of the animal.

Gut Hook Skinner

The primary objective of the gut hook skinner-style blade is to keep the hunter from penetrating the abdominal cavity while dressing out the animal. Using the blade's sharp edge, the hunter makes a small cut or incision at the bottom of the abdominal cavity and then inserts the gut hook into the cut with the smooth top of the gut hook blade against the abdominal cavity. With the blade's spine against the inside of the animal, the sharp gut hook is pulled toward the animal's throat, creating a zipper effect in zipping open the skin and fur, thus allowing the hunter easier access to dressing out the game. If this knife has a drawback, it can be that many hunters need help sharpening the hook's inside edge.

Bird-and-Trout Knife

Dressing out small game animals can be even more challenging than their larger counterparts. Consequently, makers build bird-and-trout knives. Generally, such a knife sports a 3- to 3.5-inch thin, slender blade. You can find examples with both drop-point and skinner-style blades. The knife style is designed primarily for dressing birds and fish, hence the name. Generally, birds are dressed to harvest the breast meat and fish for the filet. Most hunters and fishermen or women discard the remainder of the carcasses.

Another bird-and-trout knife choice is a folder with a 2.5- to 3-inch blade. Some examples feature a blade and gut hook. The idea is to insert the hook into the bird or other small game and utilize the hook to pull out the intestines and the rest of the intestinal tract.

Terry Vandeventer offers his drop-point hunter in a 4.5-inch ladder-pattern damascus blade, a stainless guard with file-worked copper wire, sheep horn handle scales and a custom leather sheath. (Chuck Ward photo)

Blades Lengths, Materials, and Maintenance

Blade lengths are often designed to process a particular bird or animal. Smaller blades in the 2.5-3-inch range are primarily used for dressing birds. This short blade length allows the hunter to quickly extract the breast meat from the bird. The most common blade length is 4-4.5 inches, which will dress out most game hunted regularly in North America.

The Bob Loveless drop-point hunter is the world's most emulated hunting knife and features a 4-inch blade. When dressing out larger game such as moose or elk, many hunters prefer a longer blade, up to 6 inches in overall length. The idea behind a hunting knife is to dress out game without cutting into vital organs. Going much past a 5-inch blade can affect the average hunter's ability to control the edge.

Blades are primarily stainless and high-carbon steels, though damascus has gained in popularity over the years. The environment a hunter will be in, and their skill level at resharpening an edge determines the choice of steel. Each steel has advantages concerning rust resistance,

ease of sharpening and edge holding. Carbon steels such as 1084, 5160, and 52100 provide an extremely keen edge and can be easily resharpened. They do, however, require more maintenance. Stainless steels like 440C, ATS-34, and CPM 154 make up most of those used on custom hunters. These can be easier to sharpen and more forgiving regarding maintenance.

Regardless of the steel choice, the blade should be cleaned, and a light oil coating should be applied after each use. It's best not to store your knife long-term in a leather sheath, as the tannic acid in the leather can rust a blade. Additionally, leather holds moisture, which hastens the rusting process. You should store knives in something other than leather sheaths.

Diversity! If you're looking for custom knives with diverse handle materials—synthetics, wood, ivory, bone, antler, pearl, and others— hunting and utility blades lead the way.

When outdoorspeople dress a knife to impress, they want a stag handle. Unfortunately, stag is experiencing two things simultaneously, and neither is good. Because of a lack of supply, quality is decreasing, and the price is increasing to a point where fossilized ivory is now considered a viable alternative. I've started to order some hunting knives with elk antler handles for this reason. While less popular than stag, elk antler is a great handle material with a nice look.

The "Moreno Semi-Skinner" from Kurt Swearingen enlists a 4-inch, satin-finished CPM 154 blade, stainless guard and amber stag handle. It comes with a custom sheath by the maker. (Chuck Ward photo)

My experience in the field has made me a true believer in synthetic handles. The two most popular materials are Micarta and G-10. Canvas Micarta is my personal favorite. As its name implies, canvas Micarta is manufactured with canvas woven

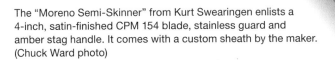

into the matrix, giving the knife handle a bit more grip when wet. Westinghouse Micarta, often considered vintage or antique because most material was made before 1960, is gaining popularity.

Carbon fiber is five times stronger than steel, twice as stiff and lighter in weight. The material enjoys numerous commercial applications and has found favor in the custom knife market, initially as handle scales for folders. Custom knifemakers have also adopted carbon fiber for

Bob Merz fashions a folding bird knife with a drop-point CPM 154 blade, a gut hook, stainless bolsters and stag handle scales. (Chuck Ward photo)

fixed blade handles.

Synthetics have the advantage over natural handle materials because they don't shrink or crack and are generally impervious to the elements. Nothing can compare to the inherent beauty of many natural handle materials.

Blade Steel

If you ask a hundred people about the best steel for a hard-use field knife, you will probably get at least two dozen different answers. Why? End users are very loyal to a steel that is proven in the field. Steels are made primarily for commercial applications, with very few explicitly manufactured for knives. Most of us have seen knife blades fashioned from saws, files, car springs and even railroad spikes. If the steel has enough carbon and can be hardened to hold an edge, someone has made it into a knife blade.

The two primary choices for knife blades are high-carbon and stainless steel. Each has its pros and cons. The most significant advantage of stainless steel is that it is corrosion-resistant and requires less maintenance. Additionally, some feel it's easier to sharpen. Stainless is not a code word for no maintenance. Yes, stainless steel will rust.

Carbon steel requires maintenance. Many things will make carbon steel rust—the blood from the game being processed, extended time in damp conditions, acids, salt or saltwater, some vegetation, and fruits and vegetables. However, the rust can be minimized or eliminated simply by cleaning and oiling the blade

Ben Breda's stag hunter showcases a 5.5-inch random-pattern damascus blade, stainless guard, sambar stag handle, copper spacer and custom leather sheath.

after use. Remember that storing a high-carbon hunter in a leather sheath, especially a wet leather sheath, can cause the blade to rust. The tannic acid used to process the leather can cause rust spots.

While carbon steel may rust, it does have advantages over stainless. If appropriately sharpened, it will hold an edge longer. Using a forged blade from a custom knifemaker will give you two more advantages. First, most makers build blades with distal tapers, thus reducing the overall weight of knives. Second, utilizing a differential heat treatment allows the blade greater flexibility.

Damascus steel has gained favorability among users over the last 15 years. This is especially true in the kitchen cutlery community.

Damascus hunters gained a foothold in the custom knife world six years ago. While many patterns are beautiful, custom knife buyers often ask why damascus is so expensive.

An American Bladesmith Society master smith once explained the cost of damascus to me like this: A starting point would be a random-pattern damascus billet. A basic 120-layer random-pattern damascus bar cut, restacked and rewelded takes 3 to 4 hours to achieve a working billet. For ladder-pattern damascus, add 2 hours to that of a 120-layer random-pattern billet. For twist damascus, add 1 hour to the ladder pattern or 3 hours to the random-pattern 120-layer billet. Creating the ladder or twist patterns results in a significant loss of steel in the process.

Some of the more unique patterns, such as feather, Turkish twist, or mosaic damascus, require a lot more steel to begin with, involve a greater risk of failure, and significant steel loss in the process of forging, grinding, and cutting to achieve a desired result. This can add 2 to 3 days of bladework. A basic random pattern can add $300 to the cost of a knife and over $1,000 for more detailed/complex patterns. Many variables, such as blade size, style and pattern choice, can affect the price.

"San mai" steel, meaning "three flat things" in Japanese, has an incredibly distinctive look. Most U.S. bladesmiths forge san mai blades to include a high-carbon core (1084 alloy) surrounded by two layers of stainless steel. This is just one example. Other materials such as copper and damascus are also incorporated into san mai blades. San mai steel requires a hardened core of high-carbon steel surrounded by stainless on each side, resulting in a durable blade with excellent edge-holding ability.

The steel utilized for a hunter's blade should be an alloy that can be sharpened in the field and meets all requirements of what the knife is designed to accomplish." Remember, it's always best to resharpen your knife before it gets dull.

Knife Guards

Most custom hunting knives are designed with a single, curved guard that enhances handle ergonomics and protects the user's index finger and hand. The primary metals for guards are brass, nickel, silver and stainless steel. Brass is proving popular among factories and new custom knifemakers. The biggest problem is that it is soft and easily nicked or marred. This can then make the guard uncomfortable against the bare hand. Stainless steel guards provide the best protection and require the least maintenance.

Building knives with integral, squared-off guards meant to protect a user's index finger and hand is generally quicker and less expensive. However, I learned that this type of guard is not meant for hard work. Therefore, wear gloves if you use a knife with this type of guard.

Summary

Choosing the correct hunting knife for your time in the field requires research. Hunting knives come in various shapes and patterns, providing options for choosing the right size, steel, and handle necessary to get the job done. It would greatly benefit outdoorsmen and women to hold a hunting knife in their hand for sizing. You must always be able to control the blade edge. Remember, the rifle or bow harvests the game, but the knife creates what becomes dinner and possibly even a trophy. □

San mai is the steel of choice on a Steve Randall hunter with amber stag handle and a custom sheath. (Alison Randall photo)

A "Nessmuk Skinner" from Luk Kuberski sports a 4.75-inch Sleipner stainless steel blade in a satin finish, a maple burl handle and a custom leather sheath. (Robertson's Custom Cutlery photo)

The Sole Authors of *Knifemaking*

Controlling all aspects of the craft gives these blade builders great satisfaction.

By Rick Dunkerley, American Bladesmith Society (ABS) Master Smith

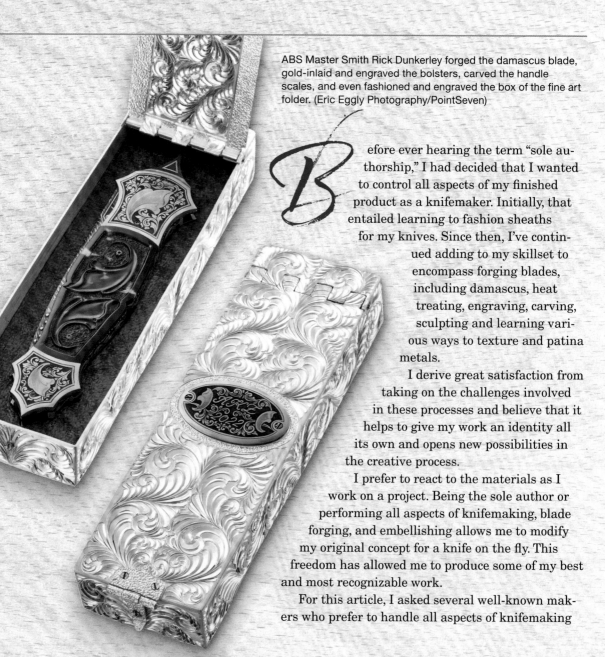

ABS Master Smith Rick Dunkerley forged the damascus blade, gold-inlaid and engraved the bolsters, carved the handle scales, and even fashioned and engraved the box of the fine art folder. (Eric Eggly Photography/PointSeven)

Before ever hearing the term "sole authorship," I had decided that I wanted to control all aspects of my finished product as a knifemaker. Initially, that entailed learning to fashion sheaths for my knives. Since then, I've continued adding to my skillset to encompass forging blades, including damascus, heat treating, engraving, carving, sculpting and learning various ways to texture and patina metals.

I derive great satisfaction from taking on the challenges involved in these processes and believe that it helps to give my work an identity all its own and opens new possibilities in the creative process.

I prefer to react to the materials as I work on a project. Being the sole author or performing all aspects of knifemaking, blade forging, and embellishing allows me to modify my original concept for a knife on the fly. This freedom has allowed me to produce some of my best and most recognizable work.

For this article, I asked several well-known makers who prefer to handle all aspects of knifemaking to discuss what sole authorship means to them and how it helps define their work.

ABS Master Smith Larry Fuegen

"Historically speaking, I believe Master Bladesmith James Schmidt coined the term 'sole authorship' in the late 1970s or early 1980s. It referred to the maker performing every step of the knifemaking process by themselves. I first heard of this concept in 1984, at an ABS Hammer-in in Dubois, Wyoming, where Jim was one of the instructors.

"As a bladesmith living in Maine, I had created all my knives in this manner, and most early bladesmiths followed this concept of hand forging, grinding, heat treating and finishing their blades in their shops without any outside help. They also finished the handles and guards. For makers like me who wanted to do 100% of the work, we also made our own sheaths.

"This was the case until the maker wanted to go past the basic knife and fashion something special that involved engraving, carving, etching or other forms of embellishment. At that point, they collaborated with other artisans who offered their skills to the finished knife.

"True believers of the sole authorship concept continued to master the skills of engraving, carving, working with precious metals, etc., to create their knives and maintain total artistic control of their work. I'm proud to say that each piece that leaves my shop is a sole authorship knife. It makes no difference if it is a basic hunter or a unique art knife. The only exception is the two knives I've done that were in collaboration with other makers for fundraisers or special gifts."

Jordan LaMothe says he enjoys working in a wide variety of media and techniques, from forging damascus blades to engraving, carving, and leathermaking. (SharpByCoop photo)

Dellana's "Major Meltdown" art folder is dripping with damascus, gold, pearl, and jewel inlays, with all the work done by the artist, including making the knife parts.

ABS Master Smith Harvey Dean

"I made my first knife in 1979. My blades were made by the stock removal method until 1984, when I began forging. Around 1988 or 1989, I forged my first damascus blade. All that time, I was making my own steel, doing my own heat treatment and then performing all the other work myself, so my knives were considered sole authorship. I liked having control over my product from start to finish.

"As time went on, I began wanting to make more high-end and embellished knives. I began working with several engravers, which resulted in some of my work no longer being of sole authorship on these pieces. The problem I ran into with this is scheduling and coordination. If I wanted to take a knife to a show with engraving on it, I had to finish it quickly so that the engraver had time to complete their part of the project before the show. Many times, it seemed I was rushing myself and the engraver also. There were times that the deadline could not be met.

"In August 2007, I attended the GRS engraving school in Emporia, Kansas, and took a class under the instruction of my friend, Steve Dunn. After a couple of years, I felt confident enough to offer my engraving if the client preferred it. I was now able to achieve sole authorship again.

If gold-inlaid, engraved damascus push daggers with mammoth ivory handle scales are your thing, then Harvey Dean is your man, and he'll create the entire knife and even embellish the piece.

Rick Eaton's sole authorship folder showcases a gold-inlaid damascus frame, engraving, black-lip mother-of-pearl inlays, and a forged damascus blade.

Larry Fuegen engraved, carved and sculpted the art dagger, fashioning and embellishing a throat-and-tip sheath for the piece.

"I enjoy doing the entire project, making it all mine. In addition, if the project is not completed in time, it is on me and no one else. I also like the challenge of learning and accomplishing new things.

"In 2021, I took a one-on-one class with another friend of mine, Barry Lee Hands. Now, I can offer raised gold overlays. I think it is cool to learn things from other people, whether it be forging damascus, engraving or carving. Then, when I do the work, I try to put a bit of myself into the process, so the knives and embellishments always look a little different."

Dellana

"I was intrigued when I first heard the great ABS Master Bladesmith Jim Schmidt say he was a sole authorship knifemaker. I had not heard the term before. He went on to explain that it meant that he forged his own damascus and did all the other work on his knives. I loved the concept of this and aspired to become a 'sole authorship' knifemaker myself. As a goldsmith [pre-knifemaker], I had always loved to learn and master different metalsmithing techniques, so this was right up my alley.

"How does sole authorship pertain to my work? I forge the damascus steel for my blades, make all parts and mechanisms for my knives, as well as do all the gold and silver fabrication, stone setting, engraving, etc. Having this control over all phases of the process is important to me as a knifemaker and an artist.

"I find that most of the makers who create sole authorship knives tend to pay incredible attention to detail and have a desire to continue improving their technical skills in order to present the best knife they are capable of creating."

Rick Eaton

"Why sole authorship? There are many great artists who combine to make great pieces, but there are only a few mak-

ers who took their skills to create another level of art by controlling the beginning foundation of a knife, as Jim Schmidt did, by also making the damascus, or performing all finishing aspects of a knife, like Henry Frank doing engraving as well.

"These guys were the ones who I would emulate in my knives to control the whole process and create this art. In the process, there is a continuity of thoughts, and I see a flow of creativity that can go to the next level. The only downside I see to this is the limited quantity of knives a sole authorship knifemaker can create because of the multiple jobs inherent to the process. The upside is some great knives that are hard to emulate except by only a few who devote the time to develop the skills and achieve such levels.

"Personally, I started as an engraver of my dad's knives but wanted to make knives, too. Then, after making mainly art knives for many years, learned to forge damascus after going to my first Montana

From the tip of the heat-colored damascus blade to the gold-inlaid butt of the art folder, Rick Dunkerley did all the work himself, including the engraving, carving and sculpting. (Mitchell Cohen photo)

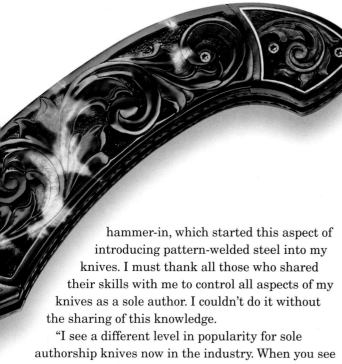

hammer-in, which started this aspect of introducing pattern-welded steel into my knives. I must thank all those who shared their skills with me to control all aspects of my knives as a sole author. I couldn't do it without the sharing of this knowledge.

"I see a different level in popularity for sole authorship knives now in the industry. When you see the knives, you'll know why."

Shaun and Sharla Hansen

"We definitely consider ourselves sole authorship knifemakers. Even though we work together on the knives, we do all aspects in-house, from design to forging the damascus to engraving and gold inlay. The knives are handmade down to the smallest screws and parts for double-action knives.

"We've been making knives full-time for 27 years and were inspired to this style of sole authorship by Buster and Julie Warenski, who invited us to their home and shop in our first year of knifemaking. They gave us guidance, direction and advice, helping us in so many ways. As sole authors, we're able to, for better or worse, control our art throughout the process.

"We've been so grateful for the knife industry, from the collectors and purveyors to fellow knifemakers and show promoters. It's been the best business, the art world, where so many have become great friends. They are the best kind of people you'll ever come across."

ABS Master Smith Jordan LaMothe

"When I am asked why I make knives, I most often reply 'because the craft enables me to work in a wide variety of media and techniques—those like blacksmithing, machining, jewelry, woodwork and leatherwork—and put them all into one final product that is both a useful tool and a beautiful object.'

"Working in different media is the hallmark of sole authorship knifemaking, and I find it has two primary benefits to me and my work. The first benefit is that making all the various components of a knife diversifies the work to be done, breaking up the monotony of any individual task.

"For instance, when I am in the middle of a lengthy grinding or sanding operation, I take comfort from the fact that the next step in working on that knife will involve forging or matching handle scales or embellishment of some kind, and I will be able to exercise a different set of skills and muscles. Diversifying my day-to-day work in this way increases my enjoyment of the craft as a whole. I believe that enjoyment is critical for both producing quality work and sustaining a career over the long term, both of which benefit makers and clients alike.

"The second benefit of making sole authorship work is that the maker retains complete control of the design process from start to finish, leading to an end-product that is unified in its conception and design.

"Each of my knives starts with an idea, which I typically refine by sketching, drawing and modeling the different shapes before making it in its complete form. Because I am both the designer and maker, I can allow the design process to continue as I craft the piece, making small edits to the design as I go. Each of these edits is an opportunity to improve the final piece without compromising the work or vision of others, an important consideration if one is working with collaborators."

Conclusion

As you can see, there is a common theme among the makers of sole authorship knives. Control of the project from start to finish and the desire to push themselves to learn new and challenging skills are a common denominator for all who graciously contributed to this article. As for myself, I can tell you that there is no greater satisfaction than stepping back and looking at a completed project, knowing that I made the whole thing, good or bad, all me. □

Knives
ARE IN OUR DNA

Our tool, craft, passion and legacy, the knife is ingrained in us as human beings.

By Ernest Emerson, Emerson Knives

Prehistoric examples of ancient knives from the author's collection date to circa 1.5 million years BCE.

here's just something about knives. From the dawn of human civilization, the knife has been an indispensable tool, serving as an extension of our hands and an embodiment of our ingenuity. The knife's evolution traces the very progress of human society, with each edge and contour reflecting the needs, beliefs, and aspirations of diverse cultures across the ages. Beyond its practical applications, it has taken on many symbolic roles in historical, cultural, military, and religious contexts, weaving a fascinating tapestry of human existence.

An article done several years ago posed a simple question to a prestigious panel of noted academics, scientists, researchers, and historians, along with over 3,000 other participants. The question was, "What are the top 20 tools ever created by man throughout all human history?" Can you guess the number one ranked tool over all that man had ever

developed, the hands-down winner? It was the knife.

Historically, it is also one of the first tools, if not the first, ever created by man. Now, picking up a stick is one thing. But breaking off a piece of rock to create a sharp edge you can use requires both finite skills and forethought. And at least for the moment, archeological research credits one of our distant ancestors named *Homo Habilis* (handyman or toolmaker) with being the first proto-human to "flake" rocks into the first cutting tools. So, about 2 million years ago, the first knife was born, and recent evidence now seemingly pushes the date back another million years or so.

Looking back through the mists of time, let's imagine this. An ancient relative of ours came upon a downed animal. He might've thought, "Alright, I've got some food, but how do I get at it?" Animal skins and hides, especially those of a mammoth, woolly rhinoceros, or bison, were extremely thick, tough, and

An official issue Gurkha kukri from the author's collection is pictured on a regimental commander's hat.

covered in dense fur, with the meat attached to bones, ligaments and tendons. Only a knife would enable that ancient relative to get to the good stuff.

And ever since that long-forgotten time, the first-born of necessity—a knife—has been humankind's constant companion, along for the ride with us from the arctic steppes and desert plains to the frigid vacuum of outer space and the surface of the moon. Wherever mankind has gone and wherever we shall go, our most essential and useful tool, the knife, has always been at our side.

A hammer is a tool for a carpenter, an axe for a woodsman, a wrench for a mechanic, a rope for a cowboy, and a stethoscope for a doctor, all useful and purpose-built for specific tasks. But none even comes close to matching the need for a good knife. What tool do we find in almost everyone's pocket or purse, from CEOs and boardroom executives to tradesmen, doctors, police officers, soldiers, farmers and ranchers to dads, moms, grandmas and grandpas? Yes, it's the knife.

Do you remember your first pair of shoes? Can you recall the keychain your first car keys were on? How about the first book you ever read? All of these are important milestones. Most people probably don't remember them all, but I'm willing to bet almost all of us remember the first knife we ever owned.

Grandpa's Barlow

Mine was a Barlow jackknife, which my grandfather gave to me on the back porch of the family farm-house when I was about eight years old. I remember Grandpa saying, "Don't tell your mom or grandma. It'll get me into trouble."

I remember everything about that moment. My grandpa, his worn blue coveralls, the sunlight on us, the feel of the cement steps we were sitting on and the homemade plumbing-pipe railing behind him. And I remember the knife, every detail of it. It wasn't new because it was one that he had carried for quite a while. And now it was mine. I miss my grandpa and that knife. They're both gone, and I certainly wish I

Each of the unit insignias bears a knife in its official design.

still had them in my life.

The knife is truly the ultimate, universal tool, but it is not just a tool. It is such a necessity that we use one in some capacity every day of the year. It's an integral and essential part of our daily routine, from the kitchen to the job site, places, and times needed to rescue someone or save a life. And yes, a knife is even used for fun. Just ask any whittler.

Long after mankind has perished from this earth, what will remain behind? Mozart will be gone. Skyscrapers will be lost to time. The earth will take back bridges and roads. The pyramids might be left, and perhaps Mount Rushmore. But I know one thing will remain: the original flint and obsidian versions of mankind's oldest, most useful and valuable tool, the knife. Besides some scraps of crumbling fossilized bones, knives are the only contemporary evidence proving mankind's history of existence going back millions of years.

Why do we make knives? Why do we collect them and feel such an unexplainable attraction to them? Although we all feel this way for many reasons, there is one answer to both. I believe it's in our DNA.

I also believe in genetic memory, and I'm convinced that over those 3 million years or so, the knife has ingrained itself into our very makeup. Knives and their place in our evolution are bound to us over countless generations. We don't have claws or fangs, so we created knives. And those edged creations allowed us to survive as a species.

Speaking for myself about making and collecting knives, I can only say that I do the things I love. If I can, I'll still collect and make knives until the day I die, and I know I'm not alone in that feeling.

From a broader perspective, the cultural significance of swords and knives has been evident across various civilizations. In medieval Europe, the sword became a symbol of knighthood and chivalry. Bestowing a sword upon a knight was a powerful ceremony, representing honor, loyalty, and the responsibility to protect the weak. In this context, the sword embodied the ideals of a noble and just society.

Soulful Extension

In Japan, the katana holds a revered place in history and culture. Beyond its practical use in samurai warfare, the katana was seen as a soulful extension of the samurai himself. The forging of one was considered an art form, with each sword having its unique characteristics. The samurai's code, Bushido, emphasized the spiritual connection between the warrior and his sword, elevating the weapon to a status beyond a mere combat tool.

Like the one shown, the author's first knife was a Barlow jackknife given to him by his grandfather on the back porch of the family farmhouse when he was about eight years old.

Similarly, the kukri knife of the Gurkhas in Nepal is not just a utilitarian tool but rather a symbol of the Gurkha warrior's bravery and loyalty. Carrying the kukri is a tradition passed down through generations, representing the Gurkha's commitment to duty and honor.

In Scandinavia, the seax, a type of single-edged knife, held deep cultural significance. Vikings considered their seaxes not just tools but extensions of themselves, often adorning them with intricate runes and symbols. The tribal name "Saxon" is derived from the association of Norse culture as "men of the seax."

The Scottish sgian-dubh, a small knife traditionally worn in the sock, represents a blend of utility and symbolism. It is a symbol of honor, still worn today during formal occasions such as weddings and gatherings, reflecting the wearer's connection to tradition and a warrior's heritage. Although now mainly filling a symbolic role, it's still fully functional for self-defense or utility purposes should such needs arise.

Knives and their larger siblings, swords, are also woven into the fabric of our religious and mytho-logical narratives. In Christianity, the sword is a recurring symbol, representing divine justice and protection. The flaming sword guarding the entrance to Eden and the two-edged example mentioned in the Bible as a representation of the word of God are examples of the symbolic power ascribed to these weapons. And in mythology, most people can honestly say they are familiar with the Ancient Greek myth about the "Sword of Damocles," or the sword in the stone, King Arthur's "Excalibur."

In its various forms, the knife has been an essential companion to warriors throughout history. From the Roman gladius to the bowie knife of the American frontier, such blades have become synonymous with the bravery and sacrifice of those who wielded them.

This connection between blades and identity extends to modern times, particularly in military traditions. Many military units incorporate knives and swords into their formal dress, parade uniforms and insignias and patches, reflecting a deep-seated connection to the warrior ethos. These symbols serve as a reminder of the sacrifices made, challenges faced,

and unity forged on the battlefield. As a tool and weapon, the knife becomes a badge of honor and a link to the lineage of those who served before. It's not just a Ka-Bar. It's a Marine Corps Ka-Bar.

We might all agree that the knife is a testament to the human species' ingenuity, creativity and adaptability. Its journey through time mirrors our evolution from primitive survival to sophisticated artistry. Across cultures and contexts, the knife has become more than a tool; it is a symbol of identity, protection, sacrifice, legacy and spirituality.

Dad's Old Hunting Knife

My dad passed away several years ago, and he left me just a few things, including his hunting rifle. But my most prized possession of all? His beat-up, old hunting knife. I still see it in his hands whenever I pick it up and hold it. It kindles so many fond memories.

Whether in the hands of a chef, a soldier, a collector, or a grandfather, the knife tells a story, a narrative of human experience etched into our collective memory, our very soul, and I, for one, believe in our DNA. And, as we continue to shape our world and navigate the ever-increasing complexities of existence, the knife remains a steadfast companion, a silent witness to our triumphs, struggles and enduring spirit. I believe it will stand beside us faithfully and always— until the end of our watch. □

Left: The official model issued to the International Space Station (ISS), Emerson Knives Incorporated blades have been to outer space and back.

Right: An authentic mid-12thcentury medieval crusader sword from the author's collection (left), found near the city of Acre on the Mediterranean coast of the Southern Levant. The Roman sword (gladius) at right dates to the mid-2nd century AD and was found in what was ancient Dacia, now modern Romania.

TRENDS

The knives are talking again. They tell so much if you take the time to pay attention. The materials talk, too, often telling knifemakers what patterns of knives to make. More than a few blade builders have openly discussed how inspiration often comes from the materials they've gathered over the years. They pick up a piece of stag, a slab of ivory or a scale of canvas Micarta, and a knife design comes to mind, one that flows with the pattern, shape or size of the material. They build knives around the materials.

Once the knives are built, the bladed beauties speak to collectors and enthusiasts, beckoning them to pick up the edged tools, weapons and works of art and handle, look and feel. The knives tell the users what to cut, how, and using which motions. There are many clues as to what the blades are designed to accomplish—the knives' historical significance, lengths and shapes, weight, curvature, thickness and balance.

Some are modern folding knives, and others are "Lordly Swords," classic fixed blades, "Huntsmen's Quarry," Native American weaponry, "Bangin' Bowies," or "Whetted Foodie Ware." Many are "Works in Westinghouse Micarta" or part of "The Synthetic Handle Movement." These are the Trends in knives. They emerge after the materials have spoken to the makers, and the resulting knives have beguiled collectors and users.

The Synthetic Handle Movement

ndustrial ingenuity at its finest combines with custom knife craftsmanship to give us some of the hottest handle materials this side of a spacecraft, which, in the case of the Apollo 11 Command Module, had glow-in-the-dark discs partially made from refined nuclear waste inside the exterior hatch handles so astronauts could find them in the pitch-black atmosphere.

None of the knife handles in this chapter contain radioactive discs inside, but some look like they do, or at least lava, mint, cherry ribbons and chocolaty goodness. The truth is that material suppliers have gotten awfully creative with their grip offerings to the benefit of knifemakers, users, enthusiasts and collectors.

Regulations on ivory, horn, stag, tortoiseshell, and even some pearls are partially to blame for the synthetic handle movement, but complaining does no good. Unless African elephants and Galapagos Island tortoises start breeding like rabbits, the regulations aren't going away.

With the beauty of modern synthetics, the knife industry might survive such natural disasters. And, well, there's always refined nuclear waste if push comes to shove.

« RYAN FORBES:
Kirinite acrylic handle scales anchor the "Element Cleaver" featuring a thick, groovy CPM 3V blade.
(Mitchell D. Cohen Photography)

» TOM BULLOCK:
The maker added phenolic handle scales from an antique bowling ball to go with the CuMai blade of a Lanny's Clip-style slip-joint folder.
(BladeGallery.com photo)

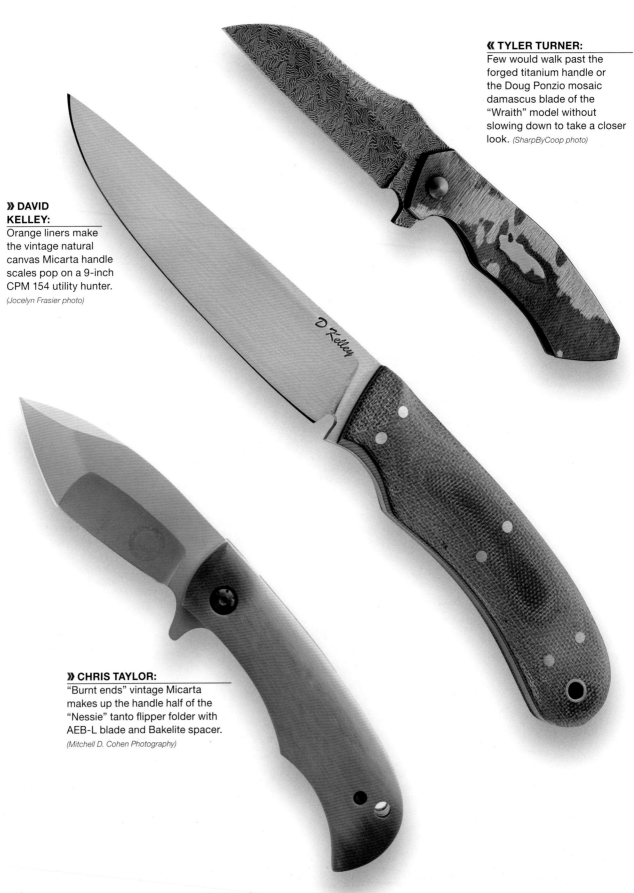

» TYLER TURNER:
Few would walk past the forged titanium handle or the Doug Ponzio mosaic damascus blade of the "Wraith" model without slowing down to take a closer look. *(SharpByCoop photo)*

» DAVID KELLEY:
Orange liners make the vintage natural canvas Micarta handle scales pop on a 9-inch CPM 154 utility hunter.

(Jocelyn Frasier photo)

» CHRIS TAYLOR:
"Burnt ends" vintage Micarta makes up the handle half of the "Nessie" tanto flipper folder with AEB-L blade and Bakelite spacer.

(Mitchell D. Cohen Photography)

» CHRIS RICHARDSON:
Clean lines and mint green
G-10 handle scales define
the CPM Magnacut folder.
(SharpByCoop photo)

⌃ DREW LININGER:
Jade G-10 makes for
a good first impression
on a tanto Kwaiken with
an AEB-L blade and
titanium guard.
(Jocelyn Frasier Photography)

« TOM MAYO:
"Dr. Death" comes calling
in CarboTi and Damasteel.
(Mitchell D. Cohen Photography)

« DAVID JESSIE II:
The handle half of a CPM 154 trekker/hunter/utility knife is sculpted camouflage G-10.
(Mitchell D. Cohen Photography)

» JASON KNIGHT:
The 80CrV2 "Fett Tanto" is handled in green over black over red G-10. *(SharpByCoop photo)*

» GEORGE BAARTMAN:
"Gold Snakeskin Fatcarbon" handle scales work their magic on an M390 wharncliffe slip-joint folder. *(BladeGallery.com photo)*

» JASON HOWELL:
The copper-inlaid forest green and red G-10 handle of the flat-ground CPM everyday carry knife is reminiscent of 1950s hotrod flames, topographical maps and early Doppler radar readouts all rolled into one. *(SharpByCoop photo)*

« JOHN ARNOLD:
The winning handle material combination on an M390 "Coffin Midi" front flipper is burgundy Micarta and shred carbon fiber. *(BladeGallery.com photo)*

⌃ STEVEN RAMOS:
A bead-blasted CPM 154 blade, Micarta handle, G-10 liners and digital camouflage Kydex sheath give the "Pisces" hunting/utility knife a tactical look and feel.
(Jocelyn Frasier Photography)

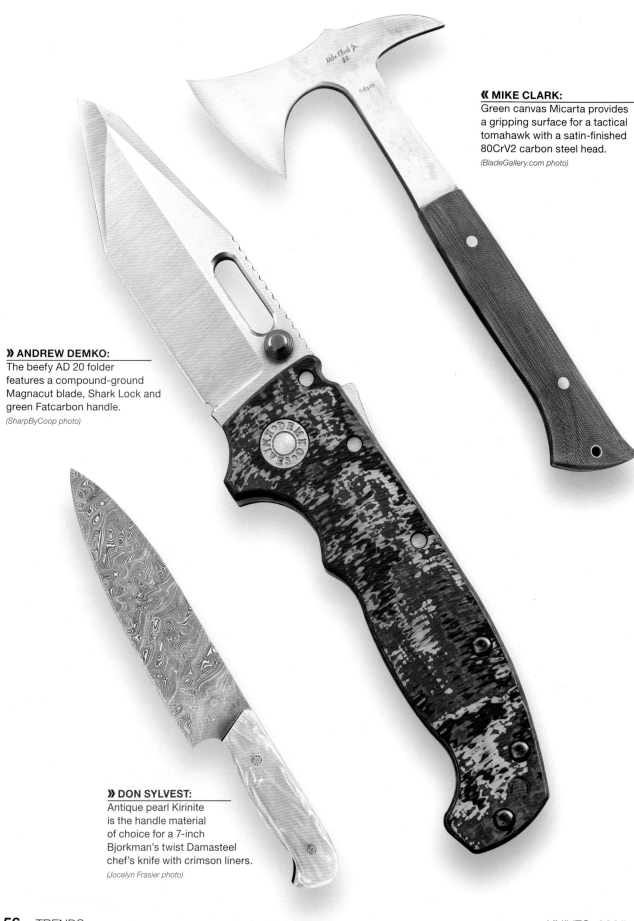

« MIKE CLARK:
Green canvas Micarta provides a gripping surface for a tactical tomahawk with a satin-finished 80CrV2 carbon steel head.
(BladeGallery.com photo)

» ANDREW DEMKO:
The beefy AD 20 folder features a compound-ground Magnacut blade, Shark Lock and green Fatcarbon handle.
(SharpByCoop photo)

» DON SYLVEST:
Antique pearl Kirinite is the handle material of choice for a 7-inch Bjorkman's twist Damasteel chef's knife with crimson liners.
(Jocelyn Frasier photo)

» DMITRY SINKEVICH:
A titanium frame-lock folder parades "Summer Coordinal" Carboquartz inlays, a hand-rubbed, satin-finished RWL-34 blade, and a multi-row bearing system.
(Mitchell D. Cohen Photography)

« FRANCOIS DU TOIT:
Red Fatcarbon is the handle material of choice for the maker's spectacular Damasteel folding tanto.
(SharpByCoop photo)

« NOAH SMITH:
While Vegas Forge "Shark's Tooth" damascus makes up the business end, a Fatcarbon handle finishes off the piece.
(Mitchell D. Cohen Photography)

» JON MOORE:
The aptly named "Cherry Ribbon" polymer handle is a bow atop the gift, a 7-inch, random-layered damascus hunter/skinner.

⌄ PETER CAREY:
Red CarboQuartz gets top billing as the handle for a "Venture" flipper folder with a Chad Nichols Intrepid damascus blade. *(Mitchell D. Cohen Photography*

« CHARLES COOK:
A stripe of colorful G-10 runs through the cedar handle of a damascus, extended-tang, slip-joint folder with a brass frame.
(SharpByCoop photo)

⌃ ED SOL:
A bowie knife is the beneficiary of a "Twilight" Corian handle, brass guard, and AEB-L blade.
(Mitchell D. Cohen Photography)

≋ J.W. RANDALL:
The Louisiana maker dresses his latest utility knife in 1080-and-15N20 damascus and two-color Micarta. *(SharpByCoop photo)*

》 DANIEL KOERT:
Vintage blue Micarta makes a statement on the "Pershing" folder that showcases a Mike Norris hybrid damascus blade.
(Mitchell D. Cohen Photography)

》 MIGUEL NAVARRO:
The handsome handle combination is vintage Micarta and desert ironwood, accompanied by a 3-inch, hollow-ground Hitachi White san mai blade and red and black G-10 spacers. *(SharpByCoop photo)*

》 MAL HANNAN:
A recurved, bead-blasted D-2 utility fixed blade is fittingly handled in black linen Micarta. *(Rod Hoare photo)*

« IAN HOLEY:
Holey collaborated with friends Drew Lilinger and James Arnold on the Damasteel kitchen knife with blue marbled carbon-fiber handle and ivory Micarta liners.
(Mitchell D. Cohen Photography)

« BRIAN MILINSKI:
Calling it a "random carbon-fiber handle with copper liners," the maker's damascus fighter is the better for it. *(Jocelyn Frasier Photography)*

» SHAWN SHROPSHIRE:
The practical tactical enlists a forged 80CrV2 blade and Fatcarbon "Orange Lava" handle scales. *(SharpByCoop photo)*

« RYDER HARTLEY:
"Arctic Storm" carbon fiber is the cold, hard handle material of an AEB-L double-edged "Nightmare"-ground fixed blade.

(Mitchell D. Cohen Photography)

⨺ JACO DE KOCK:
Faux ivory is a safe bet for the handle scales of a "Kazi" flipper folder in a stainless Damasteel blade and Timascus bolsters.

(BladeGallery.com photo)

⨠ JAMES BUCKLEY:
Modern materials include a Rob Calcinore mosaic damascus blade, a Red Dark Matter Fatcarbon handle, and a MokuTi thumb stud and standoffs.

(Mitchell D. Cohen Photography)

« ERIK MCCRIGHT:
The maker file-worked the frame around the vintage Micarta handle of a W2 fighter with visible hamon (temper line).
(Jocelyn Frasier Photography)

» TREVOR BURGER:
A frame-lock front flipper is maxed out in a hand-rubbed, satin-finished Elmax stainless blade and Blue Dark Matter Fatcarbon handle scales.
(BladeGallery.com photo)

» GEOFFREY BAZE:
A blacked-out kukri is the beneficiary of a butterscotch Micarta handle.
(Jocelyn Frasier Photography)

《 CRAIG HOOK:
With an Utem thermoplastic and
Dark Matter carbon-fiber handle
on one end and a Chad Nichols
"Starfire" damascus blade on the
other, the folder is one sharp package.
(Mitchell D. Cohen Photography)

》 JARED OESER:
The sharp "Tachi" group
is executed in blue Micarta
and damascus.
(Mitchell D. Cohen Photography)

Native American Weaponry

As distinctly unique as the clothing, jewelry, art and artifacts of indigenous peoples of North America, their edged tools and weapons are instantly identifiable. Having recently perused the book *The McKenney-Hall Portrait Gallery of American Indians,* I was reminded of just how many of the Native American war clubs, sheath knives, daggers, tomahawks and pipe tomahawks that knifemakers replicate today were first studied in reproductions of the portraits and biographical sketches commissioned by Thomas Loraine McKenney to document a comprehensive history of North American Indians.

Many knifemakers are familiar with the book containing reproductions of original Charles Bird King oil portraits that were unfortunately destroyed in an 1865 fire at the Smithsonian Institution. The valuable portraits were part of a government collection featuring prominent Indian leaders who visited Washington, D.C. Several knifemakers have referenced the book over the years, as many tribal leaders chose to pose for their portraits wearing or holding their edged tools and weapons.

With historically accurate replication a goal of many knifemakers, such illustrated references are invaluable insights into the distinctly stylish Native American weaponry.

⌃ JOSH BLOUNT:
A frontier hunter has a low-layer twist damascus blade, sheep horn handle scales, rawhide accents and copper liners and ferrule.
(Jocelyn Frasier Photography)

» RUSSELL ROOSEVELT:
The enticing damascus tomahawk features silver wire inlay in a highly patterned wooden haft.
(SharpByCoop photo)

» JARROD FISCUS:
In the intimidating spontoon tomahawk style, the curly maple haft features domed pins and feathers to go along with the SAE 4147 half pike.
(SharpByCoop photo)

» SHAWN SHROPSHIRE:
A 20.5-inch frontier bowie is executed in a Go-Mai damascus blade, mild steel guard and fossil walrus ivory handle.
(SharpByCoop photo)

Funereal Coffin Handles

Dust swirls up from the dirt road; the camera pans back, allowing the viewer to see the street of a Western town, wood plank sidewalks, a lady holding up her long floral dress, the fringes of her bloomers showing as she crosses from one side of the main drag to the other, storefronts seemingly built in a hurry all look the same, a scene out of a movie, muted, almost tragic. Leaning up against the clapboard exterior of one proprietary business is a coffin, the top slightly askew, waiting for the next victim.

Overromanticized? Don't tell knifemakers that. The coffin-handle bowies, daggers and fixed blades within conjure up such imagery and more: dust-covered chaps, silver spurs, boots that have seen years of wear over unforgiving land, a leather sheath extending nearly to the knee of a cowboy riding the range. Within the leather scabbard is a bowie knife, a long-bladed extension of the need to survive, to eat, drink, shelter, wash and work.

Coffin-handle bowies are as romantic as a damsel in distress, a hero picking her up from the dirt on that main drag, swinging her onto the back of his saddle as he rides out of town, leaving misery behind and perhaps a few corpses lying in the road—devastation, anger, grief. Funereal coffin handles evoke all those emotions and more, perhaps even eliciting a knowing smile or two from the makers.

» CHRIS BERRY:
Behold the "Coffin Ranger," complete with a Magnacut blade, green linen Micarta handle scales, and bone-white linen bolsters.
(Mitchell D. Cohen photography)

« HARVEY DEAN:
This dagger's going out in style, complete with a fossil-walrus coffin handle, gold cross, gold guard inlay and damascus blade. *(SharpByCoop photo)*

» JAMES INGRAM:
The bowie pays its respects dressed in 80CrV2 steel and curly maple. *(SharpByCoop photo)*

« NICK BACHTEL:
A gentleman's coffin-handle dagger is orchestrated in 1084 high carbon steel, bronze and buckeye burl. *(SharpByCoop photo)*

« GREG COKER:
In the words of the maker of the dagger, "I flew AH-6 Little Bird gunships in the 160th Soar. I was shot down in Iraq while supporting Delta Force on March 19, 2004. The mini-gun barrels from my AH-6 were gifted to me, and I forged the mini-gun barrels and World Trade Center steel, also given to me, into the 1,600-layer damascus blade." *(SharpByCoop photo)*

» SHAYNE CARTER:
Laid out for your viewing pleasure is a coffin-handle damascus bowie with one of the prettiest mammoth ivory handles in all the land and heavens above. *(SharpByCoop photo)*

⌃ CHRIS GARDNER: :
The flat-ground W2 bowie boasts a coffin-style mammoth ivory handle. *(SharpByCoop photo)*

« SAM LURQUIN:
A fitting tribute to Bill Bagwell, the differentially heat-treated bowie/fighter sports a coffin-style ironwood handle and domed brass pins. *(SharpByCoop photo)*

Lordly Swords

» JEFFREY WAGENAAR:
Mosaic "Puzzle" damascus
and camel bone add to the
mystique and grandeur
of the impressive sword.
(SharpByCoop photo)

**« RUCUS
COETZEE:**
A medieval arming
sword enlists a hand-
forged, gun-blued
5160 blade, antique
wrought iron guard, and
stabilized and
dyed maple burl hilt.
(BladeGallery.com photo)

« GEOFF KEYES:
Walnut, bronze, copper
and steel are assembled
for the greater good of
a 34-inch gladius sword.
(Jocelyn Frasier Photography)

» BILL MILLER:
The Japanese-inspired short swords sport damascus blades and blackwood and bird's-eye maple hilts.
(Mitchell D. Cohen Photography)

« JOHN HORRIGAN:
Taking a wide berth around the 26-inch hunting sword might be advisable with this model in a Turkish-twist damascus blade, red sambar stag handle, and 24k-gold leaves on the case-hardened 1045 guard.
(SharpByCoop photo)

« MATT GASKILL:
The fact that the maker calls it a "Brisket Sword" is reason enough to add the W2 long blade with smoky temper line, Koa wood handle and Micarta spacers into the mix.
(Jocelyn Frasier Photography)

» MATT PARKINSON:
The Wootz hunting sword with damascus clamshell guard, silver hilt, stingray skin grip and pronounced blade fuller will shiver the timbers. *(SharpByCoop photo)*

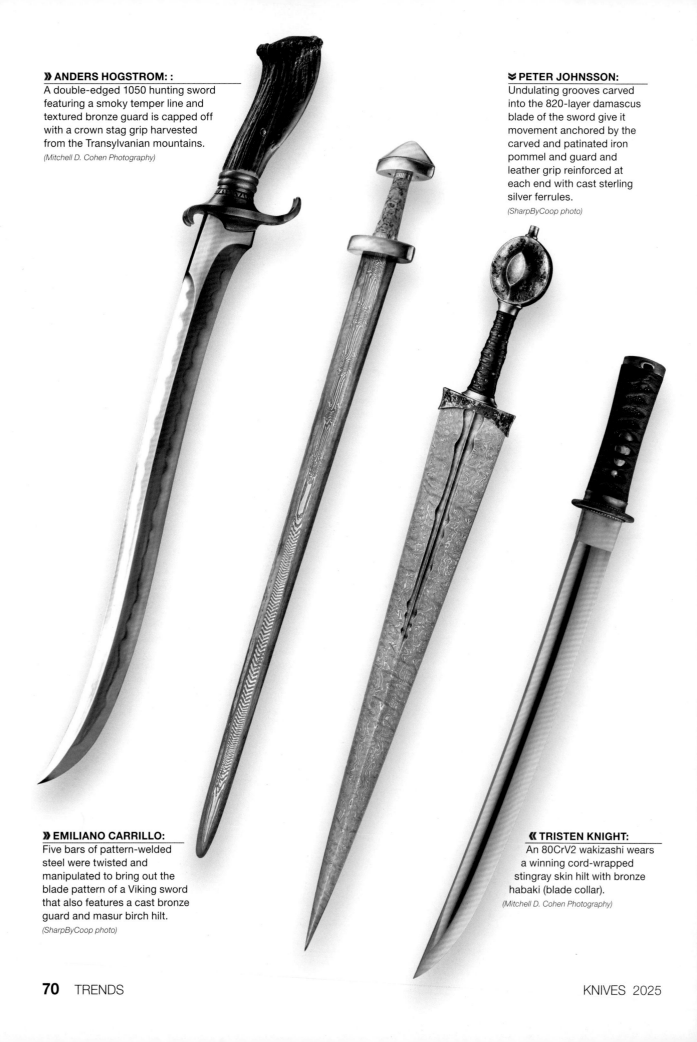

» ANDERS HOGSTROM: :
A double-edged 1050 hunting sword featuring a smoky temper line and textured bronze guard is capped off with a crown stag grip harvested from the Transylvanian mountains.
(Mitchell D. Cohen Photography)

» EMILIANO CARRILLO:
Five bars of pattern-welded steel were twisted and manipulated to bring out the blade pattern of a Viking sword that also features a cast bronze guard and masur birch hilt.
(SharpByCoop photo)

⌄ PETER JOHNSSON:
Undulating grooves carved into the 820-layer damascus blade of the sword give it movement anchored by the carved and patinated iron pommel and guard and leather grip reinforced at each end with cast sterling silver ferrules.
(SharpByCoop photo)

« TRISTEN KNIGHT:
An 80CrV2 wakizashi wears a winning cord-wrapped stingray skin hilt with bronze habaki (blade collar).
(Mitchell D. Cohen Photography)

» DENIS TYRELL:
The "Silver Moon Katana" is accomplished via a damascus-over-pure-silver laminated blade with an 80CrV2 core, silver fittings and inlay, a mild steel guard, and wrapped stingray skin hilt.
(Jocelyn Frasier Photography)

« VINCE EVANS:
Piercing, engraving, gold inlay, carved walnut Celtic knotwork, and a 33-inch damascus blade are highlights of a Scottish basket hilt sword.
(SharpByCoop photo)

« DALE WINBURN and JASON KNIGHT:
The "Night Wanderer" sword is executed in ladder-pattern damascus, a wrought iron, bronze and copper guard, bog oak handle, gold plating and blue sapphires.
(Mitchell D. Cohen Photography)

» J.W. RANDALL:
The impressive hunting sword showcases a 22.5-inch "Texas Wind" damascus blade, stainless guard, blue walrus ivory handle and Alice Carter engraving.
(SharpByCoop photo)

» MICKEY YURCO:
A Philippine marines sword enlists a 7.25-inch, full-tang, hollow-ground, etched 440C blade, ivory G-10 handle scales, carbon-fiber pins and lanyard hole.

(Mitchell D. Cohen Photography)

» TOM CARROLL:
A damascus Viking sword looks robust in brass, bone and iron.

(Mitchell D. Cohen Photography)

⌃ JACCO VAN DE BRUINHORST:
The dagger and sword set is skillfully accomplished in eight-bar damascus, twisted silver wire, wrought iron, Norwegian bog oak and gold.

(SharpByCoop photo)

The Rise of Resin Fusion

Two things are going on here—resin and fusion—in addition to incredible workmanship, blade making, design and execution.

Fusion is trending not only in the materials industry but also in restaurants and food service, fashion, design, art and architecture. Urban areas of the world feature Mexican/Caribbean, Cuban/American, Thai/Western, Korean/barbecue and Vietnamese/Thai fusion cuisine in restaurants that blend culinary traditions and techniques from different cultures into tasty food.

Fusion in modern art embodies the spirit of an interconnected globe where many customs, races and cultures influence artists. Fashion fusion is a blend of traditional and contemporary styles.

As far as colored resins are concerned, they've been melted and poured into channels and gaps of wooden tables, lamps, desks and chairs to create hardened lakes, rivers and patterns that wind through the grains of wood and add splashes of color.

Modern knife handle materials combine resins with other synthetic materials, often creating brilliant arrays of stunning colors, textures and palpable patterns. The rise in resin fusion has taken the materials industry by storm, and knifemakers and enthusiasts have benefited.

≪ MIGUEL NAVARRO:
The AEB-L Kwaiken features a Juma "Golden Snakeskin" resin handle with red G-10 liners and mosaic pins. (SharpByCoop photo)
(Mitchell D. Cohen Photography)

≪ BRANDON VALLOTTON:
The "Divinity" switchblade combines a Baker Forge Copper Mai blade and Dichrolam (dichroic film and hard resin) "Dragon Burl" handle scales. *(Mitchell D. Cohen photography)*

» ANDY ISAACKS:
A 3.5-inch, mirror-polished AEB-L hunter is treated to a hybrid ringed Gidgee wood and resin handle with black liners.

(Jocelyn Frasier Photography)

« KYLE VALLOTTON:
A Voodoo Resin "Nuke Flower" handle makes a splash on the Executioner auto with Chad Nichols Boomerang damascus blade and bolster.

(Mitchell D. Cohen Photography)

» RANDY LEE:
The fine fixed blades come in California buckeye burl, ironwood, and bronze and pinecone resin.

(SharpByCoop photo)

Modern Folding Knives

« CASEY MIDDLETON:
A Persian frame-lock folder dons a Nitro V blade and titanium handle frame.
(Mitchell D. Cohen Photography)

« JEREMY KRAMMES:
With a Magnacut blade, a titanium frame and a G-10 handle, this one sings a modern tune.
(SharpByCoop photo)

« REESE WEILAND JR.:
The "Street Fighter Slipper" flipper folder enlists a two-tone CPM 154 blade and a titanium frame with abalone inlay.
(Jocelyn Frasier Photography)

» TREVOR BURGER:
The frame-lock front flipper has a hand-rubbed, satin-finished Elmax stainless blade, a machined titanium handle, and a black Timascus pivot collar and back bar.
(BladeGallery.com photo)

⌃ KIRBY LAMBERT:
Meet Augustus, the full-dress flipper folder who wears a CTS-XHP blade with temper line, zirconium bolsters, MokuTi pivot collars and carbon-fiber handle scales.
(Mitchell D. Cohen Photography)

» BARRY BARNARDT:
The "Ozee" front flipper is designed with a carbon-fiber handle and RWL-34 blade.
(BladeGallery.com photo)

⌃ KIRK MAYBERRY:
A mokume-gane handle and two-tone acid-washed CPM 154 blade highlight the Fatboy flipper folder.
(Mitchell D. Cohen Photography)

❯ JACO DE KOCK:
Damasteel, titanium and Timascus comprise the bulk of the "Kazi" frame-lock front flipper.
(BladeGallery.com photo)

« BRIAN BROWN:
The modern tanto folder marries a ZircuTi frame with a Damacore-powdered metal blade.
(Mitchell D. Cohen photography)

≫ WILFRED VALTAKIS:
"Stitch" is a sharp Borka Blades M390 folder in a patriotically engraved titanium handle. *(SharpByCoop photo)*

≫ TOM MAYO:
A super Damasteel hawkbill folder is handled in CarboTi.
(Mitchell D. Cohen Photography)

» ERIC LUTHER:
The "Sancha M" flipper folder has a Zirblast bead-blasted CPM 154 blade and titanium frame, the latter with "speed holes."
(Mitchell D. Cohen Photography)

» JOHN BARKER and LEE WILLIAMS:
Black Timascus adds a splash of color to the "Slantine Kickstop" in a CTS-XHP blade.
(Mitchell D. Cohen Photography)

» EMMANUEL ESPOSITO:
Gold dots accent the carbon-fiber handle scales of a sharp Double C-Lock folder.
(Mitchell D. Cohen Photography)

« KURT MERRIKEN and IAN TYSON-PICKARSKI:
The Karma folder gives off good vibes via `````'s hollow-ground, hand-rubbed Armor Core blade and a Chad Nichols Dark-Ti handle.
(Mitchell D. Cohen Photography)

« JEREMY MARSH:
The "Mini Whisper" speaks in hushed tones of white Timascus, Damasteel and yellow pearl.

(Mitchell D. Cohen Photography)

« A2—ANDRE VAN HEERDEN and ANDRE THORBURN::
The flipper folder features a "Lightning Strike" carbon-fiber handle and a double-row ceramic IKBS (Ikoma Korth Bearing System).

(BladeGallery.com photo)

« EVAN NICOLAIDES:
The "Stingray" slip-joint CPM 20CV folder sports a dimpled and anodized titanium handle frame.

(Mitchell D. Cohen Photography)

« ANDREW DEMKO:
Featuring the maker's "Shark Lock" mechanism, the AD-22 model also sports a 3-inch, hollow-ground Magnacut blade and a titanium handle frame.

(SharpByCoop photo)

» CHRIS TAYLOR:
Aside from the blue acorn shield, the folder is all black, including a Chad Nichols "Boomerang" damascus blade, titanium liners and canvas Micarta handle scales.

(Mitchell D. Cohen Photography)

⌄ BOB MERZ:
A small auto and a back-lock folder showcase CPM 154 blades, pearl handle scales and engraving by Wes Griffin.

(SharpByCoop photo)

« ALEX HOSSOM:
The "Primo" folder is as curvaceous as it is clean, including the multi-ground blade and OD green G-10 handle scales.

(Mitchell D. Cohen Photography)

» TASHI BHARUCHA:
The "Crook" (top) and "Baby SOS" folders have cutting-edge designs and materials, the latter being titanium and RWL-34 steel.

(Mitchell D. Cohen Photography)

« BOB TERZUOLA and TRACKER DAN:
Bob's ATCF flipper folder marries an acid tumble-finished blade ground by Tracker Dan with a notched thumb rest, anodized titanium frame and black silk-wrapped stingray skin handle.

(Mitchell D. Cohen Photography)

» YI HUANG: :
The "Aires" front flipper relies on a Bertie Rietveld "Nebula" damasacus blade, crushed paper Micarta handle scales, titanium liners and a forged back spacer.

(Mitchell D. Cohen Photography)

⌃ K.C. GRAY:
The "Tombstone" flipper folder features a Damasteel Damacore tanto blade, vintage emerald Micarta handle scales and Timascus and titanium fittings.

(Mitchell D. Cohen Photography)

⌃ DARRIEL CASTON:
The sculpted Balisong boasts a CPM S90V blade and a lot of machining, sanding and finishing (blood, sweat and tears?).

(SharpByCoop photo)

« CHAD NELL:
A clean switchblade is handled in carbon fiber and G-10.
(Mitchell D. Cohen Photography)

« LUCAS BURNLEY:
Modern and classic collide on the "Tuna" CPM 154 frame-lock folder with a titanium frame and jigged bone handle inlays.
(Mitchell D. Cohen Photography)

« JENSEN BERGMAN:
Break out the Brewtool2 in a Magnacut blade, canvas Micarta handle with wood inlays and a ZircuTi clip.
(Mitchell D. Cohen Photography)

» BRYAN MONTALVO:
The wicked-looking "Cross Breed Folder" combines Chad Nicols Magnacut damascus, titanium and ZircuTi.
(Mitchell D. Cohen Photography)

» D.R. DAVIS:
A fresh take on a Lanny's Clip model, the folder parades a titanium handle polished with a lightning finish and a CPM 154 blade.
(Mitchell D. Cohen Photography)

« HERUCUS BLOMERUS:
A modern "Rhino" flipper folder features an SG-2 Takefu blade, a superconductor pivot and a full-scale SG-2 handle.
(SharpByCoop photo)

« EYAL LANDESMAN:
It took a mirror-polished RWL-34 blade to compete with the titanium frame in a frosted finish and mother-of-pearl handle inlays.
(Mitchell D. Cohen Photography)

To-Die-For Fighters

« STEVE GATLIN:
The one-two punch of a 12-inch fighter consists of CPM 154 steel and mammoth ivory.
(SharpByCoop photo)

» LIN RHEA:
An impressive Karambit is wrought from 80CrV2 steel and anodized titanium.
(Jocelyn Frasier Photography)

» DEON NEL:
A snakewood-handle fighter in N690 steel is a sleek and sexy number.
(SharpByCoop photo)

« RUCUS COETZEE:
A Naval dirk is dressed to the ebony and twisted brass wire hilt in an antiqued brass guard and a hand-forged 5160 blade with a gun-blued finish.
(BladeGallery.com photo)

» DIETMAR KRESSLER:
Pearl pretties up an integral Big Bear sub-hilt fighter in the style of the late, great Bob Loveless.
(Mitchell D. Cohen Photography)

« JAKE SUMMERELL:
A Japanese sika deer antler handle does its best to hold back an integral fighter's 100-layer random damascus blade.
(Rod Hoare photo)

» NATHAN CAROTHERS: :
An otherwise black linen Micarta-handle CPM 3V fighter is outfitted with blue screws for a little lift.
(SharpByCoop photo)

« RICK EATON:
A mosaic damascus Mediterranean fighter showcases arabesque engraving, full relief carving and a takedown buffalo horn handle.
(Francesco Pachi Photography)

» JERRY HOSSOM:
The "Reprisal" fighter enlists Russian damascus and ivory Micarta.

(Mitchell D. Cohen Photography)

« SCOTT GALLAGHER:
The "Argyle Fighter" has a blacked-out 80CrV2 blade, blackwood handle and hot-blued guard.

(Jocelyn Frasier Photography)

« CHRIS HAMELIN:
A Wolfgang Loerchner design, the 440C fighter exhibits a muskox horn handle, cherry red G10 liners and a brass bolster.

(Jocelyn Frasier Photography)

« BRIAN NAWROCKI:
The musk ox-handle 1095 fixed blade with brass S-guard has some fight left in it.

(SharpByCoop photo)

» ERIK MCCRIGHT:
The fighter hits the ring with an 8-inch 52100 blade, Richlite handle, nickel-silver guard, and file-worked frame.
(Jocelyn Frasier Photography)

« JAMES INGRAM:
The prizefighter is of takedown construction and showcases a W2 blade, blued-steel guard, and ironwood handle. *(SharpByCoop photo)*

» ROBERT APPLEBY:
The Loveless-style Dixon fighter comes at you in a CPM 154 blade, an amber-dyed elk antler handle, and red fiber liners. *(SharpByCoop photo)*

⌃ STACY HALL:
A clean bowie blends a flat-ground 52100 blade, stabilized myrtle wood handle, and a mild steel guard and pommel.
(Rod Hoare photo)

« PEDRO GONZALEZ:
As pretty a fighter as one is likely to find, it sports a 7.5-inch "Diamond Copper-Mai" blade by Baker Forge and Tool, a faux horn bolster, and an old-growth redwood burl handle. *(Jocelyn Frasier Photography)*

» TRISTEN KNIGHT:
The "Wraith" is ready to wreak havoc via an 80CrV2, nickel and wrought iron san mai blade, burl handle, and a crown stag pommel carved in a skull motif with G-10 and bronze eyes.
(SharpByCoop photo)

« CHAD NELL:
A stealth sub-hilt fighter is clad in green canvas Micarta.
(Mitchell D. Cohen Photography)

» SAM LURQUIN:
Featuring a G-10 handle carved by Serge Raoux and a guard engraved by Elisabeth Da Justa, the 18-inch fighter is a dominating damascus force. *(SharpByCoop photo)*

⌃ JARRETT CIESLAK:
The large 24-inch Reape bowie/fighter enlists a 1084-and-15N20-damascus blade, a curly myrtle handle, and bone file work.
(SharpByCoop photo)

» DON PENNY:
One of the most handsome fighters in his class, the 300-layer, four-bar twist damascus model has a shock of blonde claro walnut handle.
(Jocelyn Frasier Photography)

» GARY LANGLEY:
Engraved and gold inlaid by Bertram Edmonston IV, the classically styled Loveless fighter features a mammoth ivory handle and stainless guard. *(SharpByCoop photo)*

« MACE VITALE:
The rough forged W2 blade and curly oak handle are configured into a to-die-for fighter.
(SharpByCoop photo)

Whetted Foodie Ware

Foodie is a relatively recent addition to the English language, dating from the early 1980s. It indicates a person having an avid interest in the latest food fads. According to mashed.com, the term originated in 1980 when Gael Greene used it in *New York Magazine*.

The latest food fads come and go, but custom chef's knives and other handmade kitchen cutlery belong to a category that has remained hot for several years. There is a commonality between foodies and collectors and users of custom chef's knives, though, in that they all appreciate the finer things in life. A person doesn't usually pony up for handmade kitchen cutlery unless they intend to prepare fabulous food.

It comes down to quality—of the food, knives, and the overall experience. People the world over have learned to appreciate the warmth and comfort of cooking and entertaining in their kitchens. They want to make the experiences memorable, and some beautifully fashioned Foodie Ware is just the meal ticket. Yes, nothing whets the collector's appetite quite like Whetted Foodie Ware.

《 MATT WILLIAMS:
Which chef's knife is for you? Size differential apart, the damascus and san mai pieces with spalted pecan handles and mesquite dowels make for a fine pairing.
(SharpByCoop photo)

» FRANCOIS MAZIERES:
The Sabatier kitchen knife is orchestrated in a low-layer damascus blade, a scalloped, pinned and soldered guard, and a eucalyptus burl handle.
(Rod Hoare photo)

⌃ ADAM KLUMB:
Between the temper line on the 26C3 blade and the figuring of the dyed box elder burl handle, the 7-inch chef's knife has character and movement.
(Mitchell D. Cohen photography)

« JIM ARBUCKLE:
A big ol' 11.6-inch meat cleaver sports a snakeskin sycamore handle. *(BladeGallery.com photo)*

» NICK EDWARDS:
An integral, convex ground, Western-style damascus chef's knife is handled nicely in rosewood.
(Rod Hoare photo)

» ALFREDO FACCIPIERI:
Damasteel and curly maple are a killer combination for the K-tip chef's knife.
(Jocelyn Frasier Photography)

⌄ ERIK GREINER:
The 10-inch chef's knife comes in a double-stabilized Karelian birch handle and a rough forged 80CrV2 blade.
(SharpByCoop photo)

» MICHAEL ANDERSSON:
The multi-bar damascus slicer is the proud recipient of a reindeer antler handle.
(BladeGallery.com photo)

« JEFF GRAZIOPLENE and SAM EVANS:
The integral chef's knife is a Japanese/Western hybrid of silver steel, African blackwood, G-10 and nickel. *(Jocelyn Frasier Photography)*

⌃ BILL OGDEN:
When in the market for a good paring knife, one needn't look further than the stainless damascus model in desert ironwood, bronze and giraffe bone. *(SharpByCoop photo)*

» MARK CORDINA:
A Honyaki slicer is perfectly executed in a differentially heat-treated W2 blade, an African blackwood handle, and stippled bronze spacers.
(Rod Hoare photo)

« AIDAN GARRITY:
A C-ground Nakiri has a forged 1095-and-15N20 damascus blade, a carbon fiber and G-10 bolster, and an Elforyn (faux ivory) handle.
(SharpByCoop photo)

« BROCK WOODSON:
A winsome mosaic damascus chef's knife features solid brass brazed to its spine and a water buffalo horn handle.
(Jocelyn Frasier Photography)

« BEN AKIN:
It's all ironwood, AEB-L stainless and sharp.
(BladeGallery.com photo)

» CASEY VILENSKY:
A spacer of mammoth tooth separates the Koa handle and colossally cool carbon damascus blade of a Gyuto chef's knife.
(SharpByCoop photo)

« ARYEH GOLDENSON:
A Hawaiian Koa handle counterbalanced the deeply etched and polished Chad Nichols stainless blade.
(Mitchell D. Cohen Photography)

» BILL BURKE:
A 15,000-layer damascus chef's knife is prepared using an African blackwood handle, silicon bronze spacers, and a muskox horn bolster.
(BladeGallery.com photo)

» BILL TYC:
The patina lines on the 52100 blades of the chef knife and cleaver were created with simple mustard, which creates a nice visual and gives a moderate amount of protection against further oxidation.
(SharpByCoop photo)

» JAKE HINTZE:
Go ask the neighbor if you can borrow her 18-inch brisket slicer in a san mai damascus blade with 80CrV2 core, maple burl handle and mammoth tusk bolster.
(Jocelyn Frasier Photography)

⌃ THOMAS FRANKLIN:
The winning recipe includes a "Jelly Roll" mosaic damascus blade, carbon-fiber handle, and ivory G-10 collar. *(SharpByCoop photo)*

« NATHAN ROENNFELDT:
An entry into the vegetable cleaver category showcases a hollow 1020 handle and a 15N20-and-1095 damascus edge.
(Rod Hoare photo)

» SILAS BLACKLOW:
Stirring up the pot is a foot-long chef's knife in a 15N20-and-1084 damascus blade and a dyed and stabilized burl handle with twisted wire accent. *(SharpByCoop photo)*

» ERIK FRITZ:
The 52100 "Petty Chef's Knife" showcases buckeye burl handle scales and stainless bolsters.
(Jocelyn Frasier Photography)

⌃ MICAH DUNN:
The key ingredients of an integral chef's knife are a ball-bearing feather damascus blade, a spalted maple burl handle, and a vintage Micarta spacer.
(Jocelyn Frasier Photography)

« DAVID JACOBSON:
When it comes to a wood handle, the maker prefers you choose a burl for your 1095 chef's knife.
(SharpByCoop photo)

≫ RICHARD COOPER:
Save me a chef's knife in a CuMai blade, stabilized blackwood handle, and copper and G-10 spacers, please.
(Rod Hoare photo)

≫ JESSE HU:
With a W1 tool steel blade and a nice temper line, the classic integral chef's knife boasts a ringed Gidgee wood handle and a brass spacer.
(Jocelyn Frasier Photography)

≫ BRIAN MILINSKI:
The 9-inch damascus chef's knife features a one-of-a-kind turned walnut "cigar" handle complete with a custom label.
(Jocelyn Frasier Photography)

» JORDAN BUCKLEY:
Hold onto that maple burl handle. You're in for a wild ride with the 8.3-inch damascus blade of an integral chef's knife.
(BladeGallery.com photo)

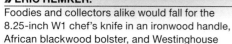

» ERIC HEMKER:
Foodies and collectors alike would fall for the 8.25-inch W1 chef's knife in an ironwood handle, African blackwood bolster, and Westinghouse Micarta spacer. *(SharpByCoop photo)*

⌃ NICHOLAS ORR:
The twist-damascus integral chef's knife with box elder burl handle will whet the whistle before a meal.
(Jocelyn Frasier Photography)

⌃ DE WET VAN ZYL:
The super mosaic damascus san mai chef's knife with O1 core comes in a brass ferrule, and a stabilized maple burl and mammoth molar handle.
(BladeGallery.com photo)

» MATT PARKINSON:
The mosaic damascus chef's knife with stainless damascus bolster and burl handle is a masterwork.
(SharpByCoop photo)

⌃ JACKSON RUMBLE:
The dazzling damascus pattern of the African blackwood-handle chef's knife might just match the table runner.
(SharpByCoop photo)

⌃ JONAS JOHNSSON:
The forging, profiling, redwood lace burl handle and sheath of the Damasteel chef's knife were crafted by Johnsson, while Japanese artisan Naohito Myojin completed the blade grind. Modern Cooking (moderncooking.com) organized the collaboration in partnership with Bonsai Boys Trading.
(SharpByCoop photo)

Bangin' Bowies

» RIAN DOUDLE:
A red gum handle anchors the 10-inch multi-bar damascus bowie blade. *(Rod Hoare photo)*

« J.W. RANDALL:
The ladder-pattern damascus blade of the bangin' bowie is paired nicely with a sambar stag handle.
(SharpByCoop photo)

» ANDERS HOGSTROM:
The temper line, blade clip, bronze guard and stag handle are all tantalizingly tempting.
(Mitchell D. Cohen Photography)

« MICHAEL ANDERSSON:
Propelled forward by a beautiful damascus blade, the bowie comes in a clamshell guard and mammoth ivory handle.
(BladeGallery.com photo)

» SCOTT GALLAGHER:
Fossil walrus ivory and 80CrV2 steel make up the handle and blade halves of an 11.5-inch bowie.

(Jocelyn Frasier Photography)

« STEPHAN FOWLER:
The recurved bowie is brought to life in ladder-pattern damascus, stainless steel and sambar stag.

(SharpByCoop photo)

» FOREST "BUTCH" SHEELY:
A Tim Hancock-style cowboy bowie hits the range in a 1095-and-15N20 damascus blade, ancient walrus ivory handle, and damascus and stainless fittings.

(Mitchell D. Cohen Photography)

« LIAM WALLE:
One "Sirius Bowie" is served up in a 7.9-inch, 970-layer "Dogstar" damascus blade, a Pohutukawa burl handle, file-worked brass liners, and a blackened "Firestorm" damascus guard, spacer, and frame.

(Jocelyn Frasier Photography)

» SCOTT HALL:
This big head-turning bowie/fighter hits the market in a Doug Ponzio Turkish lace damascus blade, Mike Sakmar mokume-gane guard, fossilized walrus ivory handle and mosaic pins.
(Mitchell D. Cohen Photography)

« MACE VITALE:
The classic bowie brings its game via a double-fullered W2 blade and a red crotch oak handle. *(SharpByCoop photo)*

» JAKE KRZENSKI:
A smoky temper line traverses the bowie blade, complemented by a copper guard, giraffe bone handle and carbon-fiber spacer.
(Mitchell D. Cohen Photography)

» BEN AKIN:
With ladder W's-pattern damascus blade, ancient walrus ivory handle, and damascus guard, the bowie will brighten your day.
(Jocelyn Frasier Photography)

« HARVEY DEAN:
Raised 24-karat gold leaves highlight the "Tejas" bowie in a fluted fossilized walrus ivory handle and ladder-pattern damascus blade. *(SharpByCoop photo)*

» JIM POLING:
A recurved Koa-handle bowie boasts a twist damascus blade, guard, spacers, pommel, and finial nut, all made from the same steel.
(Jocelyn Frasier Photography)

« RICK PILERI:
The san mai bowie sports a raindrop damascus guard and Koa wood handle.
(Mitchell D. Cohen Photography)

» JAYMES STEVENS:
It's relatively easy to like the "Lawless Bowie," blending an 81-layer damascus blade and a stacked-leather washer handle.
(Jocelyn Frasier Photography)

» LIN RHEA:
The 17-inch damascus bowie is a bruiser, boasting a stag handle, stainless guard, and a half-carat ruby on the clamshell frog of the sheath.
(SharpByCoop photo)

» JOSH HULTS:
With a highly figured ironwood handle and nickel-silver and bronze fittings, the business end of the bowie is 8 inches of 80CrV2 steel.

(Jocelyn Frasier Photography)

⌃ RUCUS COETZEE:
Blessed is the owner of a hand-forged 1075 bowie in a curly maple handle, blued-steel guard, and copper and antiqued steel spacers. *(BladeGallery.com photo)*

» BUTCH DEVERAUX:
The beastly Wyoming bowie is low-temperature forged, triple-hardened and tempered and comes in 52100 steel, brass and sheep horn.

(SharpByCoop photo)

« FRANCESCO PICCININ and DENIS MURA:
This bangin' bowie displays a smoky temper line along its 7.75-inch C130 blade and a spalted maple handle with G-10 spacers.

(Jocelyn Frasier Photography)

» JASON FRY:
The handle of the Fred Bear Bowie is fashioned from a 1966 Bear Kodiak recurved bow and accompanied by a multi-bar damascus blade with arrowhead imagery forged into the steel.
(SharpByCoop photo)

« JEREMY YELLE:
The bowie sports a Turkish-twist damascus blade, mammoth ivory handle, textured nickel-silver accents, and blued damascus fittings. *(Jocelyn Frasier Photography)*

» JAMES INGRAM:
A bronze S-guard lies between a modified ladder-pattern damascus blade and walrus ivory handle.
(Jocelyn Frasier Photography)

« SIMONE MILANESI LACANTINA:
The rare mosaic damascus bowie is packaged in a Fatcarbon guard and rosewood handle.
(SharpByCoop photo)

» JACOB ANSTAETT:
While the W2 blade does the shimmy, the Honduran rosewood handle busts some moves of its own. *(SharpByCoop photo)*

» JEAN-PIERRE POTVIN:
The "Sheriff Edition Bowie" showcases a foot-long 80CrV2 blade, maple burl handle, and brass fittings.
(Jocelyn Frasier Photography)

» ERIK MCCRIGHT:
The ABS journeyman smith's forged bowie boasts a wood handle and file-worked bronze guard.
(Mitchell D. Cohen Photography)

« JACOB GAETZ:
Starting with 1084 and 15N20, maple burl, and wrought iron, the maker arrived at a bangin' bowie.
(Jocelyn Frasier Photography)

» STACY HALL:
A clean bowie blends a flat-ground 52100 blade, stabilized myrtle wood handle, and a mild steel guard and pommel.
(Rod Hoare photo)

« JOHN HORRIGAN:
Built with wood from the Deaf Smith Oak in Austin, Texas, the bangin' bowie boasts 1095 blade steel and brass furniture. A few days after Mexican troops tried to retrieve a cannon from the Texans at Gonzales, in 1835, Erastus "Deaf" Smith climbed up the oak tree to get a better view of the countryside and spy on the Mexican troops camped on Cibolo Creek. *(SharpByCoop photo)*

» GEOFF KEYES:
The stainless damascus bowie blade is counterbalanced by a leather, Micarta, and crown stag handle.
(Jocelyn Frasier Photography)

Pocketknives with Purpose

» STEVE HOEL:
The purpose is whittling, and the three-blade beauty parades black-lip mother-of-pearl handle scales.
(SharpByCoop photo)

« JIM DUNLAP:
With congress pocketknives originally designed for shaping quill pens and whittling, the maker's example in CPM 154 steel and amber stag would suffice at such and much more.
(Jocelyn Frasier Photography)

« JASON RITCHIE:
With a handle, in this case, jigged and dyed bone, designed for a secure grip, the saddlehorn pocketknife provides extra leverage needed to puncture, cut or trim layers of tough leather.
(Mitchell D. Cohen Photography)

≫ BEN CHAMPAGNE:
A classy and classic two-blade trapper parades CPM 154 blades, stainless bolsters, and hand-checkered African blackwood handle scales.
(SharpByCoop photo)

≫ SHAWN MCINTYRE:
The 52100 blade of the amber-jigged bone-handle Barlow pocketknife is ideal for utilitarian jobs such as cutting plastic, wire insulation and thread.
(Rod Hoare photo)

≫ EVAN NICOLAIDES:
The mammoth ivory-handle AEB-L multi-blade sleeveboard pocketknife can slice a string, open a wine bottle, punch leather and file a nail with equal aplomb.
(SharpByCoop photo)

≫ DAVID KRAMP:
Whether used for pruning shrubs and flowers or as a carpenter's blade for coping, the five-blade AEB-L congress pocketknife will do, here in mammoth ivory handle scales and 14-karat rose gold pins.
(Jocelyn Frasier Photography)

≪ PAUL KILBY:
This folder blows—no, really, that's its purpose, as a harmonica knife fashioned for John Popper of Blues Traveler and including a black hollow-ground AEB-L blade.

(Mitchell D. Cohen Photography)

≫ DARRIEL CASTON:
Inspired by the split-handle folding knives of Barry Wood, the Imp keychain knife is ideal for everyday carry.

(SharpByCoop photo)

≫ JOEL CHAMBLIN:
Checkered pearl gives a five-blade Congress whittler a little jolt.

(Mitchell D. Cohen Photography)

≫ DANIEL KEOWN:
The smoker's trapper has all the necessary implements for cleaning out the pipe and tamping down tobacco, and it comes with mammoth ivory handle scales.

(SharpByCoop photo)

» TOM PLOPPERT:
A five-blade premium stockman prototype sports a 4.25-inch main blade, integral liners with milled blade reliefs, and stag handle scales.
(Mitchell D. Cohen Photography)

⌃ MATT COLLUM:
Pruning branches is a pleasure via the claw-like CPM 154 blade while gripping the RJB jigged mahogany handle.
(SharpByCoop photo)

⌃ EUGENE SHADLEY:
The pretty three-blade whittler parades mother-of-pearl handle scales and a gold shield. *(Mitchell D. Cohen Photography)*

⌃ STANLEY BUZEK:
Not your ordinary stag-handle trapper, the CPM 154 beauty showcases Alice Carter bolster and shield engraving.
(SharpByCoop photo)

⌃ BUBBA CROUCH:
Stunning is the trapper in Mike Norris stainless damascus blades, mammoth ivory handle scales, and stainless springs and bolsters.

(Jocelyn Frasier Photography)

⌃ TANNER COUCH:
Behold the upland bird knife, complete with CPM 154 blade, choke tube tool and bird cleaning hook, as well as sambar stag handle scales. *(SharpByCoop photo)*

⌃ TIM ROBERTSON:
The clean lock-back whittler sports CPM 154 blades, stainless bolsters and stag handle scales. *(SharpByCoop photo)*

» LUKE SWENSON:
Any trapper would proudly carry the CPM 154 muskrat folder in mammoth ivory handle scales.

(Mitchell D. Cohen Photography)

⌃ RHIDIAN GATRILL:
The lock-back whittler would do the job on Grandpa's front porch, executed here in CPM 154 steel blades and ironwood handle scales.

(SharpByCoop photo)

« BOBBY HOUSE:
The doctor's knife is in and looking good in CPM 154 steel, sambar stag, and pinched stainless bolsters. *(SharpByCoop photo)*

« JEFF HAWKINS:
The CPM 154 multi-blade folder with stainless bolsters and stag handle slabs is a sporting good time.
(SharpByCoop photo)

⌃ BILL RUPLE:
Any cattleman worth his salt would love to own the CPM 154 folder in Ridgeline bone handle scales.
(SharpByCoop photo)

⌃ BRUCE BARNETT:
The sowbelly slip-joint folder features mother-of-pearl handle scales and CPM 154 sheepsfoot, spay and clip-point blades. *(BladeGallery.com photo)*

⌃ MYKEL PIPER:
Boxes, beware of the MEK cutter in a hammered-brass handle. *(SharpByCoop photo)*

Hooked on Harpoon Blades

Conjuring up images of Nordic, Alaskan, and Antarctic hunters sitting high in boats using spear-like projectiles for fishing, whaling, sealing and other oceanic activities, harpoon blades are the newest thing in knifemaking. Like clip-point blades on steroids, harpoon blades sport fins like the fish the original harpoons were meant to impale and secure in their barbs. Once hooked, fishermen and hunters pulled and retrieved the sea creatures via ropes and chains.

Not many of the knives will be used to harpoon anything, much less whales or seals. Still, the projections likely have some purpose aside from aesthetics, such as elevating or pushing cutting media aside when cutting, as defensive points, or for pounding in a pinch.

Let's face it: harpoon blades look cool and give us a feeling of man versus wild, Inuit hunter against leopard seal, Norseman harpooning lampreys and Arctic explorers chasing whales.

It's no wonder knifemakers and collectors are hooked on hot new harpoon blades.

» J.W. RANDALL:
The pronounced harpoon clip of the damascus bowie is bitingly beautiful, as is that mammoth ivory handle. *(SharpByCoop photo)*

« JAKE SUMMERELL:
The maker builds his harpoon hunter in a 100-layer random damascus blade and a Japanese sika deer antler handle. *(Rod Hoare photo)*

» JACCO VAN DE BRUINHORST:
A pair of integral keyhole knives showcase mosaic damascus blades with harpoon clips and bog oak and stabilized padauk handles.

(SharpByCoop photo)

» CHRIS GARDNER:
The EDC/hunter sports a harpoon-style 5160 blade, stainless guard and African blackwood handle.

(Mitchell D. Cohen Photography)

« PAT BIGGIN:
The maker engraved the brown canvas Micarta end-grain handles and 80CrV2 blades of his harpoon points.

Huntsmen's Quarry

» DAVID JESSIE II:
The Fair Game hunting/everyday carry/utility knife features a black Micarta handle and CPM 154 blade. *(Mitchell D. Cohen Photography)*

« STEVE SANDO:
This hot little hunter arrives in a flat ground 26C3 blade, a 416 stainless and copper guard, and an Afzelia Xylay handle. *(SharpByCoop photo)*

« FRANCESCO PICCININ:
A drop-point hunter is the beneficiary of a beautiful buckeye burl handle and 5-inch W2 blade with *hamon* (temper line). *(Jocelyn Frasier Photography)*

» ARNO BERNARD:
Walking through the woods with a warthog tusk-handle utility knife qualifies as a pretty wicked activity. *(BladeGallery.com photo)*

» TANNER COUCH:
You know you're big time when you carry this rabbit skinner into the woods, complete with ivory handle scales and CPM 154 blade. *(SharpByCoop photo)*

» JOHN SCHULTZ:
A file-worked brass spacer and traditional wood grip highlight the handsome 120-layer twist-damascus hunter. *(Mitchell D. Cohen Photography)*

« CARL MICHAEL ALMQVIST:
Mammoth ivory makes a statement on a Swedish damascus hunter. *(BladeGallery.com photo)*

» FRANCOIS MAZIERES:
Hold onto the King Billy Wood stabilized fiddleback handle, admiring the mammoth ivory spacer and that exquisite random-pattern damascus blade.

(Rod Hoare photo)

« MICHAEL DEIBERT:
A hunter enters the fray in ladder-pattern damascus and curly maple.

(Jocelyn Frasier Photography)

» SHAWN ELLIS:
The masterwork includes a convex-ground W2 blade, integral guard, and smoothly sculpted desert ironwood handle.

(SharpByCoop photo)

« SHAYNE CARTER:
A chevron-pattern damascus hunter is a handful and eyeful in amber-jigged bone handle scales.

(BladeGallery.com photo)

» PAUL PETRO:
Mosaic damascus and stag make up the bulk of the hunter with a stainless guard and butt cap and bronze spacer.
(Mitchell D. Cohen Photography)

⌄ STANLEY BUZEK:
The trappings of a traditional back-lock trapper include a CPM 154 blade, stainless liners and bolsters, and ancient mammoth ivory handle scales. *(BladeGallery.com photo)*

» BOB EARHART:
A feather damascus blade points the way for the "Spring River Hunter," donning a stag handle, hammered copper spacer, and blued-steel guard and pommel.
(Jocelyn Frasier Photography)

⌄ GERRY MICHAEL:
What a handsome hunter it is with its combination chestnut burl and mammoth tooth handle and feather damascus blade. It comes with a fractal-burnt walnut base and a juvenile mammoth tooth main accent.
(Jocelyn Frasier Photography)

» CLAUDIO and ARIEL SOBRAL—CAS KNIVES:
A "Magnum" integral hunter parades a hand-forged, recurved O1 carbon steel blade in an antiqued finish and Arizona desert ironwood handle scales.
(BladeGallery.com photo)

« JIM COFFEE:
A Turkish-twist damascus hunter is handled in stag.
(Mitchell D. Cohen Photography)

» SHAWN MCINTYRE:
Few can make 52100 and stainless steel, spalted maple, and black linen Micarta look so good.
(Rod Hoare photo)

≫ CHEVY ROBERTSON and JOHN STOKES:
Of swirls and burls, the hunters are winningly fashioned from wood and damascus.
(SharpByCoop photo)

» PEYTON RAMM:
The O1 fixed blade hunters come in black canvas Micarta and desert tan G-10 handles, as well as silicon bronze guards.
(SharpByCoop photo)

⌄ BEN AKIN:
Bog oak is a nice counterpart to a handmade hunter's 5-inch dazzling damascus blade.
(Jocelyn Frasier Photography)

» JIM PERKINS:
The full-tang, 1095-and-15N20-damascus drop-point hunter parades a colorful maple burl handle that flares out at the butt.
(SharpByCoop photo)

⌃ CHRIS HAMELIN:
The "Saratoga Hunter" is a special breed, here in a 4-inch 440C blade, a handle of Micarta and Maple Valley Richlite, and a copper bolster engraved by Wolfgang Loerchner.
(Jocelyn Frasier Photography)

» CLARENCE DEYONG:
Copper is the thread running through the hunter—a 1095 and copper blade, copper spacers, and copper braid "lightning strike" carbon-fiber handle scales.
(Mitchell D. Cohen Photography)

⌃ RUSSELL ROOSEVELT:
A sharp, pointy hunter hits the market in a ladder-pattern damascus blade and amboyna burl handle. *(SharpByCoop photo)*

⌃ STEVEN RAMOS:
A 5.75-inch, bead-blasted, hollow-ground CPM 154 blade makes up the business end of the "Gemini" hunting/utility knife handled in Micarta with blue fiber liners.
(Jocelyn Frasier Photography)

» TOM PLOPPERT:
The "Old Dog" folding hunter prototype is one Reese Bose patterned for Cattaraugus and is a tribute to Tony Bose, this in a rounded front flush joint, a CPM 154 blade that pivots on bushings, integral liners and stag handle scales.
(Mitchell D. Cohen Photography)

⌃ PAUL LEBATARD:
A finely fit, finished field and stream knife sports a 3 3/8-inch D2 blade, amber stag handle scales, and dovetailed 7075-T6 aluminum bolsters. *(Jocelyn Frasier Photography)*

» BUBBA CROUCH:
The fixed blade skinner sports a Baker Forge and Tool damascus blade, stag handle, and beaten copper bolster.
(Jocelyn Frasier Photography)

» DAVE COOK:
The 17-year-old turned stabilized maple and 1080 steel into a stout, upswept hunter. *(SharpByCoop photo)*

» ERIK MCCRIGHT:
A handsome 52100 hunter dons a vintage green Micarta handle, file-worked frame, and nickel-silver guard.
(Jocelyn Frasier Photography)

» RUSTY WAIDE:
Hunting is so much more fun when outfitted with a fly damascus blade and a blue mammoth ivory handle.
(SharpByCoop photo)

« DAVID HALL:
The damascus camp set with burl handles is ready for the trail, site, field, forest or hunting shack.
(Mitchell D. Cohen Photography)

» JIM POLING:
Damascus and quilted maple share billing on a hunter with a 4.75-inch clip-point blade.
(SharpByCoop photo)

« DE WET VAN ZYL:
The hunter stalks prey in a 4.5-inch san mai blade with a 52100 high carbon steel core, a polished bronze guard, and a stabilized Natal mahogany burl handle. *(BladeGallery.com photo)*

» JESS HOFFMAN:
A 4-inch AEB-L stainless skinner arrives in a camel bone handle at hunt camp.
(Jocelyn Frasier Photography)

» SETH PARSONS:
You won't lose the blue-handle hunter in a Magnacut CPM blade.
(Mitchell D. Cohen Photography)

« BUTCH DEVERAUX:
The left-hand Pronghorn hunter is a handsome sheep horn-handle model with a brass guard.
(SharpByCoop photo)

» MIKE CLARK:
Say hello to a san mai drop-point hunter in a spalted Asian ebony handle and stainless guard.
(BladeGallery.com photo)

» JOSH HULTS:
"Twisted W's" damascus and Bubinga wood are properly paired on a 3.5-inch skinner/camp knife.
(Jocelyn Frasier Photography)

» DR. TERRY SCHREINER:
With a stag handle repurposed from an antique serving set, the hunter also features a high carbon damascus blade, nickel-silver guard, and bronze, nickel-silver and black Micarta spacers.
(SharpByCoop photo)

» MICHAEL HOBBS:
Chechen rosewood is a new one for handle materials, here on a recurved damascus hunter with tapered tang.
(SharpByCoop photo)

» RYAN SEARLS:
The person lucky enough to get their hands on the hunting knife set takes home a pair of weathered buckeye burl-handle hunters in W2 blades with 24k gold-plated edges. *(Jocelyn Frasier Photography)*

Knife Nationalities

» CARL MICHAEL ALMQVIST:
The Swedish maker returns to his roots with a half-horn hunter in masur birch and reindeer antler.
(BladeGallery.com photo)

« MAL HANNAN:
Any Scottish Highlander worth his salt would gravitate toward the hollow-ground 440C sgian dubh featuring Phil Vinnicombe engraving on a brass guard and pommel and a fiddleback redgum handle.
(Rod Hoare photo))

⌃ ZACK TARBELL:
A design by Doug Marcaida based on the Filipino Ginunting, the "Kortada Sword" incorporates a 19-inch damascus blade and a maple handle winsomely wood burned by the maker. *(SharpByCoop photo)*

» JAVIER VOGT:
Sometimes, a maker just needs to build a Javanese kris-style auto dagger in damascus and blue mammoth ivory.
(Mitchell D. Cohen Photography)

» BAILEY COPLEY:
A Serbian cleaver is enlivened by a flat-ground 200-layer ARC Forge & Metalworks damascus blade and a ringed Gidgee handle.
(Rod Hoare photo)

⩔ MAURICIO CARLOS DALETZKY:
A gorgeous gaucho knife begins with "Dragonfly" damascus and carries on in mother-of-pearl, engraved silver, and 18-karat gold.
(Jocelyn Frasier Photography)

⩓ JIM PERKINS:
Modeled after the barong his wife used as a child in the Philippines, the maker's rendition sports a leaf-shaped, 272-layer damascus blade, copper liners, and an orange stabilized maple handle. *(SharpByCoop photo)*

» MICHAEL DEIBERT:
A Roman gladius sword showcases a low-layer damascus blade and a curly maple guard and pommel.

(Jocelyn Frasier Photography)

» TOM CARROLL:
With apparent Javanese kris influences, the "Witch" blade is a brew of bone, damascus and iron.

(Mitchell D. Cohen Photography)

⌄ ANDREW BLOMFIELD:
A keyhole gaucho knife parades an amazing mosaic damascus blade and an equally impressive river red gum handle.

(BladeGallery.com photo)

« DON FOGG:
Though retired, no one made simplistically beautiful Japanese-style, differentially heat-treated fixed blades, here with a wrapped handle, better than Don.

(Mitchell D. Cohen Photography)

» NEELS VAN DEN BERG:
The prettiest (and possibly only) Omani khanjar of the lot, it parades a low-layer twist damascus blade, bronze guard, Koa wood handle, and gold inlay, carving and engraving.

(SharpByCoop photo)

« TRISTEN KNIGHT:
A san mai damascus blade with a lengthy blood groove is an apt choice for the tanto with a traditional cord-wrapped stingray skin handle, a musk ox horn menuki (handle charm) and a wrought iron tsuba (guard).* (Jocelyn Frasier Photography)*

« MICKEY YURCO:
A Japanese-style tanto is treated to a South African bullfrog handle charm under wraps.
(Mitchell D. Cohen Photography)

« GREGORY CIMMS:
The black leather wrap over a stingray skin handle gives the tanto a dark look appropriate for the Don Hanson W2 blade.
(SharpByCoop photo)

» JASON WEIGHTMAN:
Few tantos have fossilized walrus tusk handles, but this damascus beauty does, and a Micarta bolster.
(Rod Hoare photo)

» JESSE HU:
The tanto, finished with a twist damascus blade, also features a poplar and leather handle, a brass spacer, and a copper habaki (collar).
(Jocelyn Frasier Photography)

» JOHN MEDLIN:
A worthy endeavor, the Javanese kris dagger is executed in 5160 steel, brass and wood and features "David vs. Goliath pebbles" at the base.
(SharpByCoop photo)

« KEN HALL:
An exquisitely etched 15N20 Scottish basket hilt sword features a stainless guard and a cherry hilt wrapped in twisted silver and copper wire.
(SharpByCoop photo)

» MARDI MESHEJIAN:
A 26-inch Wakizashi blends a brazen 1080-and-15N20-damascus blade with a cord-wrapped bloodwood hilt and a copper-braised diamond-plated steel tsuba (guard).

(SharpByCoop photo)

» FRANCESCO PICCININ:
Hats off to the white G-10 handle and ash burl bolster of a Nordic-style 14C28N utility hunter.

(Jocelyn Frasier Photography)

« JASON KNIGHT:
The "Brutalist Wakizashi," inspired by Tristen Knight, stretches 21 inches overall and features an 80CrV2 blade, wenge wood handle, Ito wrap and copper menuki (handle charm). *(SharpByCoop photo)*

Between the Bolsters

There could be a Trends category for every drop-dead-gorgeous handle material that knifemakers plant between the bolsters of folders.

While the business end of the knife is what counts most when the chips are down, the handle is second only in importance to the blade. Without it, all leverage is gone, and the grip area also presents an opportunity for knife artisans to create something stunning.

Nature offers many bounties—black-lip, gold-lip and white mother-of-pearl, blue mammoth ivory, the brown, red, and golden hues of burls, mastodon ivory, horn, stag, abalone, amber and more.

The natural lines, colors and contours aren't lost on knifemakers who often envision blade and handle patterns after choosing a material rather than the other way around. Whatever they're doing, they're doing it right—planting some of the prettiest materials between the bolsters of modern folding knives.

« BEN CHAMPAGNE: Bless the mini-trapper integral-frame folder with mammoth ivory inserts as it's carried on the hunt. *(SharpByCoop photo)*

« STANLEY BUZEK: Antique rag Micarta handle scales and an ivory G-10 duck shield inlay make up the handle half of a CPM 154 lock-back folder. *(BladeGallery.com photo)*

» BILL RUPLE:
Stag makes a statement on a five-blade sowbelly featuring hand-rubbed, satin-finished CPM 154 steel and a waterfall shield.

(Mitchell D. Cohen Photography)

» FRANK EDWARDS:
Mammoth ivory handle scales make their presence known on a feather damascus saddle horn trapper with mill-relieved liners and copper pins.

(Jocelyn Frasier Photography)

» SHAYNE CARTER:
A Coke bottle folder is fully realized in a ladder-pattern damascus blade, a 416 stainless integral frame and bolsters, and ancient ivory handle scales.

(Jocelyn Frasier Photography)

» PHIL JACOB:
Planting highly figured mammoth ivory between the bolsters of a file-worked slip-joint folder was pure genius.

(SharpByCoop photo)

« D.R. DAVIS:
Between Robert Eggerling mosaic damascus bolsters, the "Seahorse" whittler is awash in black-lip and white mother-of-pearl, gold, and anodized titanium.
(Mitchell D. Cohen Photography)

» TANNER COUCH:
Stag takes center stage on an upland shotgunner's knife with a CPM 154 blade, spring and 28/410-gauge choke tool and bird hook.
(Jocelyn Frasier Photography)

« JEFF HAWKINS:
Executing a four-blade congress pocketknife to perfection, the maker enlisted CPM 154, stainless steel, and amber sambar stag.
(SharpByCoop photo)

Works in Westinghouse Micarta

"The steel of the plastics industry" seems to be a fitting description for an ever-popular knife handle material that has withstood the test of time and gained adherents over the years. Developed in 1910 by Westinghouse Electric Corporation as an industrial thermo-set laminate for electrical insulation, Westinghouse Micarta is made from fiberglass canvas, linen or paper layers soaked in phenolic resin. The layers are baked and pressed into large sheets, tubes or rods of varying thicknesses.

Micarta is a hard, compact composite that will not warp, expand or shrink with age or exposure to weather. So, not only is it durable, but it has that "kitschy cool" factor with its slightly muted, mustardy-yellow looks and plastic-like shine and feel. Light enough not to feel heavy or bulky in hand, Westinghouse Micarta is strong enough for airplane propellers that won't shatter and has been used for everything from tabletops to refrigerator linings and kitchen wall paneling.

Its best use, however, is for knife handles—wonderful utilitarian edged artworks with the nostalgic looks of vintage pocketknives, fixed blades and folding straight razors.

« EDWARD RATANUN: A Westinghouse Micarta bolster separates the Mike Norris "Fire Clone" damascus blade and a curly Koa handle, giving them room to breathe. *(Mitchell D. Cohen Photography)*

» JASON RITCHIE:
The handle scales of the Rosco P. Trapper are rare, vintage, blue Westinghouse Ivorite paper Micarta complemented by a Devin Thomas stainless damascus blade and a MagnaCut spring.
(Mitchell D. Cohen Photography)

» H.L. HOLBROOK:
The clip-point utility hunter looks dashing in its vintage crosscut Westinghouse Micarta handle. *(SharpByCoop photo)*

» CRAIG BROSMAN:
Westinghouse Micarta handle scales and red G-10 liners sandwich the tapered tang of a CPM 154 drop-point hunter. *(SharpByCoop photo)*

≽ TIM ROBERTSON:
Westinghouse rag Micarta is the handle of choice for the "Haze" model mid-lock folder in a CPM 154 blade.
(Mitchell D. Cohen Photography)

» PETER CAREY:
The "Cornerstone Mini" sports a Stellite 6K blade, vintage Westinghouse handle scales with gold-lip mother-of-pearl inlay, and abalone inlays in the pivot, thumb studs, and back spacer.
(Mitchell D. Cohen Photography)

⌄ HERUCUS BLOMERUS:
The antique Westinghouse Micarta grip of a "Kolobe Flipper" folder is scrimshawed to depict warthogs in the wild. *(BladeGallery.com photo)*

⌄ WILL STELTER:
The pierced boot dagger is done up in "Twisted W's" damascus and vintage Westinghouse ivory paper Micarta. *(SharpByCoop photo)*

⌄ BRYAN MONTALVO:
The "Bull Terrier" locking-liner folder wears a Vegas Forge barrel damascus blade, Westinghouse camel and prototype Micarta handle scales, a zirconium pivot collar and Skiff cage bearings.
(Mitchell D. Cohen Photography)

» CHRIS TAYLOR:
An "Ozark Nighthawk" folder features a san mai blade, titanium liners and Westinghouse Micarta handle scales.
(Mitchell D. Cohen Photography)

⩔ IAN TYSON-PICKARSKI:
The "107 Elegant" model is aptly named for its Mike Norris "Hornet's Nest" damascus blade, Westinghouse Micarta handle and Chad Nichols Dark-Ti damascus accents.
(Mitchell D. Cohen Photography)

⩔ JESS HOFFMAN:
The "Armagh," named after a county in Ireland, sports a 3.25-inch AEB-L stainless blade, a redwood burl handle and a Westinghouse paper Micarta bolster. *(Jocelyn Frasier Photography)*

» PAUL KILBY:
The Damasteel "Alpha Shard" folder has jeweled titanium liners and Westinghouse Micarta handle scales.
(Mitchell D. Cohen Photography)

Classic Fixed Blades

The best in their fields often look to the past for inspiration. There's no sense in reinventing the wheel whenever one wants to accomplish a task. Many times, the dilemma of how to fashion the right tool for the job has already been solved by those who have gone before. In other instances, what has been achieved is so inspiring that it bears repeating.

Whatever the case, many masters of the craft have led the way and continue to inspire current knifemakers wishing to leave their marks on the industry. Whether specific knife patterns were ideally suited for the cutting chores they were designed to tackle or the handcraft and artwork were so stunningly beautiful that they positively affected modern enthusiasts, reproducing classic designs can be ultimately fulfilling.

There are enough classic fixed blades to fill books and enough tomes to fill libraries. The classics have become such for a reason. They are tried-and-true, inspired designs fashioned from hand-picked, highly fit and finished materials. One does not try to give Bach or Beethoven their own spin or pimp out a Lamborghini, but rather listen, look, touch, admire, experience, and possibly reproduce the masterpieces if there's enough talent in the tank.

The top talents in the industry meticulously crafted these classic fixed blades.

« ROBERT APPLEBY:
A classic Bob Loveless-style Big Bear Fighter comes alive in an 8.5-inch CPM 154 blade, stainless hardware, and a crown-stag handle harvested from a whitetail deer.
(SharpByCoop photo)

« JOSH FISHER:
A Samuel Bell bowie reproduction parades a ladder-pattern damascus blade and a checkered African blackwood handle.
(Mitchell D. Cohen Photography)

» EDDIE RAY:
A Bob Loveless whittler pattern involves an ATS-34 blade, stainless guard, mammoth ivory handle scales and red liners.
(Mitchell D. Cohen Photography)

⌄ BOB EARHART:
Don't tell the McCoys about the Hatfield bowie and its 278-layer ladder-damascus blade, ancient walrus ivory handle, and hammered copper spacers. We don't want to start that ruckus again.
(Jocelyn Frasier Photography)

⌃ JAMIE BISHOP:
A 14th-century stiletto reproduction features a triangular 5160 blade and a bronze guard and handle.
(Rod Hoare photo)

⌃ DR. TERRY SCHREINER:
Faux tortoiseshell, 14k-gold-plated screws, bronze liners and O1 tool steel were assembled for the greater good of a Japanese Kiridashi.
(SharpByCoop photo)

« ALEX HOSSOM:
The Doc Holiday bowie reproduction integrates wood, steel and style.
(Mitchell D. Cohen Photography)

⌃ DIETMAR KRESSLER:
An incredibly clean integral Bob Loveless-style Big Bear sub-hilt fighter is dressed in mammoth ivory handle scales.
(Mitchell D. Cohen Photography)

⌃ STEVE GATLIN:
The maker fashions a Bob Loveless-style chute knife from CPM 154 steel, desert ironwood and red Vulcan fiber liners. *(SharpByCoop photo)*

⌃ JOHN YOUNG:
It's pearl, steel and unmistakably a Bob Loveless-style New York Special. *(Mitchell D. Cohen Photography)*

» TYLER TURNER:
The maker calls it a John Wilkes Booth Replica Rio Grande Camp Knife, and she's a looker.
(Mitchell D. Cohen Photography)

⌃ MACE VITALE:
Curly oak and W2 tool steel combine on a classic bowie.
(Mitchell D. Cohen Photography)

⌃ JACCO VAN DE BRUINHORST:
In the style of a San Francisco bowie, the takedown model marries a six-bar twist damascus blade with a walrus ivory handle.
(SharpByCoop photo)

⌃ ROGER BERGH:
A half-horn puukko is the beneficiary of a multi-bar damascus blade, a buffalo horn and mammoth ivory handle, and a mammoth ivory flower inlay.
(Mitchell D. Cohen Photography)

» MATT STAGMER:
Oh, the Bill Moran bowie is so beautiful, here in 360-layer damascus, curly maple and silver wire inlay.
(Mitchell D. Cohen Photography)

» S.R. JOHNSON:
Mother-of-pearl handle scales and red liners soften the Bob Loveless-style Big Bear fighter just enough.
(Mitchell D. Cohen Photography)

» CARL COLSON:
A Bob Loveless-style New York Special features a Hawaiian Koa wood handle and a CPM 154 stainless blade.
(SharpByCoop photo)

⌃ BARRY and PHILIP JONES:
Fashioned entirely from L6 tool steel and sculpted Micarta, the boar spear is purpose designed alright. *(Mitchell D. Cohen Photography)*

STATE
OF THE ART

Looks can be deceiving. Never judge a book by its cover. In meeting most knifemakers, rarely do they strike a person as being an artist. Not that they don't dress uniquely, have a certain flair or exude style. Many do just that, and some might even carry themselves like artists. But others are blue jean- and flannel shirt-wearing men and women with work boots, rough hands and weathered faces. Still more stand behind show tables in dress clothes or casual business attire. In fact, there's no single description of knifemakers or any working group of people of the same profession. One can't generalize about a people, place or time.

Whether they look the part of artisans or not, knifemakers are fashioning some dynamic edged tools and weapons. Taking engraving tools, dental drills, hand files, heat, sandpaper, chemicals, and dyes to steel, knifemakers transform cold, hard surfaces into warm, inviting sculptures, designs and functional artistry. They choose the most highly figured burls, softest pearls, sparkly diamonds and gnarly stag for handles, the finest ivory to scrimshaw, and the hottest horn to carve.

The smithy types are striking steel and forging san mai blades and mosaic damascus. Those with elbow grease to spare are turning blades, handles and bolsters into smooth sculptures that are pleasant to the hands and eyes. The jewelers in the bunch set stones into cabochons and inlay silver and gold into guards and knife surfaces.

They shape knives "San Straight Lines," fashion "Folders That Flash," and design "Daggers to the Heart." A few even make knives from meteorites.

Knifemakers might not look or dress like artists, but they embellish blades, handles and parts to create absolute masterpieces.

« JAKE SUMMERELL: The 100-layer damascus chef's knife combines a purple heart bolster and a stabilized Huon pine handle. *(Rod Hoare photo)*

« ERIK GREINER: The rough-forged W2 blade of the chef's knife shows a smoky temper line and is accompanied by a bog oak handle with spalted oak and carbon-fiber spacers. *(Jocelyn Frasier Photography)*

All the Beautiful Burls

» CHRIS HAMELIN:
The "Lyttle Bear Fighter" boasts a vintage cable damascus blade by Brian Lyttle, a curly maple handle, and a copper guard with stainless spacers. (Jocelyn Frasier Photography)

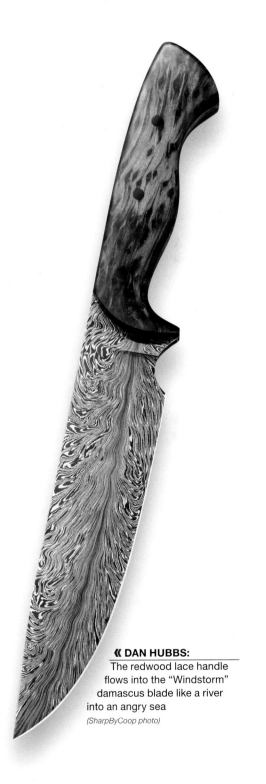

« JIM ARBUCKLE:
The maker outfits a 10.9-inch boning knife with a curly maple handle.

(BladeGallery.com photo)

« DAN HUBBS:
The redwood lace handle flows into the "Windstorm" damascus blade like a river into an angry sea

(SharpByCoop photo)

» MARK CORDINA:
Snakewood secures the 26C3 "Spicy White" blade of the Honyaki Sabatier chef's knife with a compound bevel and hidden pins.

(Rod Hoare photo)

« BRIAN MILINSKI:
A highly figured hackberry handle adds to the character of a prettily patterned stainless damascus utility knife.

(Jocelyn Frasier Photography)

» RICHARD COOPER:
Stabilized tamarind adds some graininess to a flat-ground san mai chef's knife, including a 100-layer damascus blade clad with an Apex Ultra core.

(Rod Hoare photo)

» MICHAEL RUBIN:
Cradle the curly maple handle of an 8-inch AEB-L chef's knife and let the food prep begin.
(BladeGallery.com photo)

» KELLY DALLYN:
Macassar ebony is the milk chocolatey goodness of a hand-forged, ladder-pattern damascus chef's knife with dovetailed stainless bolsters.
(BladeGallery.com photo)

» LIN RHEA:
A bowie featuring a 10.5-inch 80CrV2 blade employs an ironwood handle with forged iron fittings in a gun metal finish.
(Jocelyn Frasier Photography)

⌃ ERIK FRITZ:
Only a select few straight razors have 52100 blades and cocobolo handles.
(Mitchell D. Cohen Photography)

« TORY UTT:
The classy wedding cake service set comes in AEB-L steel, copper, and dyed masur birch burl.

(SharpByCoop photo)

» CAMILLE SENNEGON:
Wenge wood makes an appearance on a 15-inch curvaceous dagger fashioned in 1095 steel and a stainless guard.

(Jocelyn Frasier Photography)

« JON MOORE:
Stabilized Russian burl is a rarity, here as the handle of an 11-inch fighter with random-pattern damascus blade and stainless guard.

« MIKE CLARK:
Bocote wood is set on the full tang of a small hunter in 80CrV2 carbon steel.

(BladeGallery.com photo)

» LIAM WALLE:
Purple-dyed maple burl adds flavor to a Gyuto chef's knife, featuring a 3,600-layer feather damascus blade.

(Jocelyn Frasier Photography)

« A2—ANDRE VAN HEERDEN and ANDRE THORBURN:
Koa wood contrasts nicely with the black G-10 of a front flipper folder.

(BladeGallery.com photo)

» JERRY HOSSOM:
Buckeye burl gives the damascus "Bad Mike" fighter more bite than it already had.

(Mitchell D. Cohen Photography)

» RUCUS COETZEE:
The Persian dagger parades a bold ladder-pattern damascus blade, an antiqued brass bolster, and a dyed and stabilized maple burl grip.

(BladeGallery.com photo)

《 FRANCESCO PICCININ:
A northern-style utility knife
features a maple burl handle,
a 5-inch RWL-34 blade, and
G-10 spacers.
(Jocelyn Frasier Photography)

《 BEN AKIN:
Paper ivory Micarta
separates the dyed and
stabilized maple burl handle
and "Basketweave" damascus
blade of an 8-inch chef's knife.
(Jocelyn Frasier Photography)

》 MARTIN MOENNING:
Violet and teal curly maple
appear on an A2 fixed blade
with a mosaic pin.
(Mitchell D. Cohen Photography)

》 BRAD MILLMAN:
A recurved chopper is outfitted
in an 80CrV2 Brute de Forge blade
and a spalted tamarind handle.
(Jocelyn Frasier Photography)

⌃ JASON KNIGHT:
The "Bushido Chopper" is
anchored by a Koa wood handle
with a bronze spacer.
(Mitchell D. Cohen Photography)

» TAYLOR SHIELDS:
A bird-and-trout knife is clad in a 4-inch Hitachi White #1 core blade with stainless cladding, olivewood handle scales, and olive drab G20 liners.
(Jocelyn Frasier Photography)

» BAILEY COPLEY:
Stabilized she oak is a nice counterpart to a custom bowie's flat-ground mosaic damascus blade.
(Rod Hoare photo)

« RIAAN MANSER:
A curly maple inlay enhances the black G-10 handle of an H4 flipper with a hand-rubbed and satin-finished MagnaCut blade.
(BladeGallery.com photo)

⌃ PATRICK HARP:
Amboyna burl is a beautiful choice for a damascus utility hunter with a wrought iron guard.
(Mitchell D. Cohen Photography)

» RYAN SCHWARTZ:
Yellow cedar burl vies for attention versus a Bertie Rietveld damascus blade.

(Mitchell D. Cohen Photography)

« DAVID KELLEY:
Persimmon handle scales and black G-10 liners sandwich the full tang of an AEB-L kitchen and camp knife.

(Mitchell D. Cohen Photography)

« ALFREDO FACCIPIERI:
Green maple burl and hippo tooth spacers make for a fine pairing on a K-tip Damasteel chef's knife.

(Jocelyn Frasier Photography)

» JOSH HULTS:
Behold the black ash burl handle of the skinner/camp knife, here with a 3.5-inch "Twisted W's" damascus blade.

(Jocelyn Frasier Photography)

« STEPHAN FOWLER:
The handle of a ladder-pattern damascus chef's knife is a copacetic combination of Koa and dyed curly ash.

(SharpByCoop photo)

» JESSE HU:
The curly Narra handle of the K-tip chef's knife comes from the same Southeast Asian tree species as amboyna, here paired with a Don Hanson W2 blade.
(Jocelyn Frasier Photography)

« JOSE SANTIAGO-CUMMINGS:
The drop-point hunter in Chad Norris damascus combines an ironwood handle with a brass guard and black horn and composite Malachite spacers.
(Jocelyn Frasier Photography)

» JEREMY MARSH:
The combination of Koa wood and Mike Sakmar Mokume-gane puts the "Assassin" on the prowl with a claw-like Mike Norris stainless damascus blade.
(Mitchell D. Cohen Photography)

« NICK EDWARDS:
Curly maple is the sticky sweet handle material of an integral, convex-ground W2 chef's knife.
(Rod Hoare photo)

« PAUL LEBATARD:
California buckeye burl helps beautify a foot-long recurved bowie in CPM 154 steel.
(Jocelyn Frasier Photography)

« ANDREW K. SMITH:
An integral damascus Santoku kitchen knife with bronze and G-10 spacers is topped with a deliciously dyed and stabilized box elder burl handle.
(Mitchell D. Cohen Photography)

⍝ CODY ADOLPHSON:
Hawaiian Koa finds a place to shine on the "Firestorm" Turkish-twist damascus bowie with a 7-inch blade and hot-blued mild steel guard.
(Jocelyn Frasier Photography)

⌃ MYKEL PIPER:
The Damasteel "Mezo Kiridashi" features a miniritchie wood handle and vintage Westinghouse Micarta liners.
(SharpByCoop photo)

» BROCK WOODSON:
Mammoth molar and Koa wood combine to form the handle of a beautiful bowie born from a clad brass damascus blade with a mosaic core.
(Jocelyn Frasier Photography)

⌃ BRANDON HYNER:
A fixed-blade fighter combines a wave-pattern damascus blade, Koa wood handle, white G-10 guard and multi-piece spacer. *(SharpByCoop photo)*

Folders That Flash

They symbolize a fish that flashes in the water, the gleam from a sports car as it handles a curve, and the sparkle of a diamond as the lady extends her hand. They represent the finer things in life: exquisite taste, style, workmanship, and a cultured class.

Folders that flash are made with alluring materials and designs that catch both the light and the eyes of observers at levels others can only endeavor to achieve. Through impressive makeup, gentle curves, fine fit and finish, and tasteful arrangement, the folding knives leave a lasting impression on those who observe and handle them.

They are there to be picked up, used and admired. They represent engraved shotguns, carved art glass, beautiful smiles and twinkles in the eyes. They are the folders that flash, and their allure is unmistakable.

« BILL BURKE:
The "Dragon's Breath" damascus blade of the flipper folder rides on caged bearings and is complemented by titanium-damascus bolsters forged by the maker and carbon-fiber handle scales. *(BladeGallery.com photo)*

« JIM SORNBERGER:
Gold quartz and engraved gold beautifully embellish the small pocket folders.
(SharpByCoop photo)

« ANTONIO FOGARIZZU:
The gold- and pearl-embellished dagger with a stainless blade and frame is a folding firebrand.
(Mitchell D. Cohen Photography)

« ADAM ROGERS:
The six-blade stockman is a modified Case 64047p pattern executed in "Laddered W's" damascus and musk ox horn, no less.
(Rod Hoare photo)

» EYAL LANDESMAN:
Black-lip mother-of-pearl inlays are properly pieced together on the titanium handle of the Triton damascus locking-liner folder.

(SharpByCoop photo)

« MATT CHRISTENSEN:
With a Mike Norris "Fireclone2" damascus blade and Chad Nichols "Dark-Ti" scales, the "Dreadnought" flipper folder goes to battle in style.

(Mitchell D. Cohen Photography)

« A2—ANDRE VAN HEERDEN and ANDRE THORBURN:
Black Timascus enhances a Damasteel dress front flipper folder.

(BladeGallery.com photo)

« ROBERT CHAMPION:
"Comanchero" arrives at the trading post in a Jimmy Floyd carbon damascus blade, mammoth ivory handle scales, and Dale Bass gold, silver, brass and copper inlay and engraving.

(SharpByCoop photo)

⌃ EVAN NICOLAIDES:
Checkered pearl plays a prominent role on a Joseph Rodgers-style four-blade congress in AEB-L steel and threaded bolsters.

(Mitchell D. Cohen Photography)

≪ SALVATORE PUDDU:
Few have the talent or wherewithal to fashion six-blade locking folders with gold lock-back buttons, shell inlays, and 24k-gold inserts. *(Mitchell D. Cohen Photography)*

≪ BURT FLANAGAN:
A small Tony Bose-style back pocket folder is clad in Damasteel, ivory and black-lip pearl.
(Mitchell D. Cohen Photography)

≫ TYLER TURNER:
The toothpick folder features Doug Ponzio heat-blued Turkish Lace damascus, Jody Muller gold inlay and engraving on Zirconium handle scales, and an Argentium silver shield.
(SharpByCoop photo)

≫ LARRY NEWTON:
In a flash, the Doug Ponzio mosaic damascus blade flew out of the white mother-of-pearl handle into the fully open position.
(SharpByCoop photo)

≪ GARETH BULL:
The "Xyro" model is outfitted with a Damasteel blade, Timascus handle and pivot heads, and a zirconium back spacer.
(Mitchell D. Cohen Photography)

« CORRADO MORO:
Ceramic and pearl give Dracula a menacing look and feel, but one that draws you into the folding dagger. *(SharpByCoop photo)*

» JOHNNY STOUT:
A double-action feather damascus auto folder features mother-of-pearl and gold inlays and engraving by Alice Carter. *(Jocelyn Frasier Photography)*

» GUILLAUME DUCASSE:
Colorful black-lip pearl inlays enliven a double-action folder with a hand-rubbed RWL-34 blade and stainless frame. *(Mitchell D. Cohen Photography*

» BOB MERZ:
The abalone handle inlay of a damascus auto folder is enveloped by Wes Griffin gold inlay and engraving. Mike Norris is credited for the damascus. *(SharpByCoop photo)*

⌃ D.R. DAVIS:
The four-blade "Seahorse" whittler has a brilliant Timascus frame, mother-of-pearl inserts, Mike Norris damascus blades, and relieved and jeweled anodized titanium liners. *(Mitchell D. Cohen Photography)*

» RON LAKE:
A tail-lock interframe folder relies on steel, stag, and a gold bail and shield.

(Mitchell D. Cohen Photography)

» SCOTT GALLAGHER:
The "Escalante" back-lock damascus folder has a mirror-polished stainless frame with Biggs jasper stone inlays.

(Jocelyn Frasier Photography)

» TOM BULLOCK:
A sheepsfoot slip-joint folder is fashioned with a hand-ground Sandvik 14C28N stainless blade, a blue Kirinite handle and brass liners.

(BladeGallery.com photo)

« CHRIS RICHARDSON:
The Magnacut folder features a copper handle frame with a Chrysocolla TruStone inlay.

(SharpByCoop photo)

» ALAN DAVIS:
The dress locking folder arrives in a damascus blade, mammoth bark handle scales, titanium frame, and carbon steel bolsters inlaid by Tyler Poor.

(SharpByCoop photo)

» RICK EATON:
Flowing 24k-gold vines and fine silver arabesque engraving travel across the gold-lip-pearl handle of a mosaic damascus folder.

(Francesco Pachi Photography)

« JAVIER VOGT:
With a Doug Ponzio mosaic damascus blade, mother-of-pearl and zirconium handle, and gold inlays, the guard-release auto dagger is a flashy folder.

(SharpByCoop photo)

» JAMES INGRAM:
There's nothing random about the random-pattern damascus LinerLock in matching bolsters and frame and mammoth ivory handle scales.

(Jocelyn Frasier photo)

« CHRIS TAYLOR:
"Mexican Blanket Micarta" handle scales and a matching thong bead liven up a locking-liner tanto folder.

(Mitchell D. Cohen Photography)

⌄ R.B. JOHNSON:
A trio of damascus slip-joint folders features Doug Ponzio mosaic damascus bolsters, titanium liners and armadillo, fossil ivory, and mammoth tooth handle scales.
(SharpByCoop photo)

« BEN CHAMPAGNE:
Mammoth ivory and Damasteel costar on a single spay-blade saddle-horn folder.
(SharpByCoop photo)

⌃ JEREMY MARSH:
The "Black Swan" blends the beauty of Timascus and Damasteel.
(Mitchell D. Cohen Photography)

» STEVE SCHWARZER:
Inspired by the knives of Jim Schmidt, the fine folder features fossil walrus ivory handle scales and the maker's signature forged into the mosaic damascus bolsters (possibly a first in the damascus world).
(Mitchell D. Cohen Photography)

» TONY BAKER:
Exquisitely embellished by Dassa Engravings of Italy, the slip-joint interframe folder also features a 154CM blade, mother-of-pearl handle inlays and domed pins.
(SharpByCoop photo)

⌄ IAN TYSON-PICKARSKI:
A ghost-etched Damasteel blade rides on ceramic bearings, complementing a Timascus handle with a titanium inset lock.
(Mitchell D. Cohen Photography)

» MATT HUMPHREYS:
Details of a lock-back folder include scroll-engraved bolsters, mammoth tooth handle scales, and a CPM 154 blade.
(SharpByCoop photo)

« JURGEN STEINAU:
Mother-of-pearl inlay adds panache to the credit card automatic.
(Mitchell D. Cohen Photography)

« OWEN WOOD: Chevrons point the way on the damascus blade of the folding dagger, but the gold-lip pearl, damascus and gold of the handle give one pause for reflection.
(SharpByCoop photo)

« JASON RITCHIE: A Tony Bose-style Zulu Spear folder in mammoth ivory sports a hand-rubbed, satin-finished AEB-L stainless blade and jeweled stainless liners.
(Mitchell D. Cohen Photography)

⌃ HERUCUS BLOMERUS: The flashy number includes a Vinland Damasus blade, zirconium bolsters engraved by Gerhard Benade, and a ZircuTi handle.
(SharpByCoop photo)

≫ DAVID KRAMP:
Of the rare four-blade lobster ilk, CPM 154 blades and springs share billing with mammoth ivory handle scales, a double-sided banner shield, coined and jeweled liners, and black Bakelite spacers.
(Jocelyn Frasier Photography)

≪ RON APPLETON:
The clean "Corona Pass" folder sports a PSB-27 spray-formed steel blade, a PSF-27 handle frame, and a MultaLock mechanism.
(SharpByCoop photo)

≪ RICK DUNKERLEY:
Something to write home about might be a Wharncliffe folder with zirconium bolsters, black-lip-pearl scales, a ladder-pattern damascus blade, engraving, gold inlay and file work.
(Mitchell D. Cohen Photography)

≪ DAVID LONGWORTH:
It's an "Anomaly" alright, parading black-lip-pearl inlays, a rock-back blade lock, and some dynamite damascus.
(SharpByCoop photo)

Pounding Out Plumage

Feather damascus is not falling out of favor, not in the least. It's enjoying a long run and picking up steam. The train is burning up the tracks on a downward slope, full speed ahead and roaring toward destinations unknown.

I'd predict the next trend—fingerprint or snowflake damascus blades—but even though, like feathers, there are no two alike, those categories would not last. Feather damascus is a dominant industry staple because the barbs and afterfeathers of the pattern can splay out toward the edge and spine of a blade, and the rachis, or shaft, runs lengthwise down the middle. Try doing that with a snowflake or fingerprint (although, admittedly, such damascus patterning would be cool if someone wants to try it.)

Feather damascus is in a class of its own, and bladesmiths and steel suppliers are pounding out plumage faster than a grouse takes wing or a chicken lays an egg.

« ANDREW K. SMITH:
The feather damascus pattern of the curly Koa-handle chef's knife follows the blade shape from edge to spine.
(Mitchell D. Cohen Photography)

« NICHOLAS ORR:
Eye-popping patterns on the 4-inch hunter include feather damascus, quilted poplar, and jeweled bronze. *(SharpByCoop photo)*

» JOHNNY STOUT:
With a feather damascus blade forged by Bill Burke, the locking-liner folder also features white mother-of-pearl handle scales and engraving by Dale Bass.
(Jocelyn Frasier Photography).

⌄ ANDREW BLOMFIELD:
A quillon dagger is the proud recipient of a hollow-ground feather damascus blade, a gold-inlaid mild steel guard, and a fluted mammoth ivory handle with twisted gold wire wrap.
(Rod Hoare photo)

⌃ CARL MICHAEL ALMQVIST:
A Swedish utility knife combines a feather damascus blade with engraved reindeer antler and birch.
(BladeGallery.com photo)

« RICK DUNKERLEY:
Feather damascus and walrus ivory bookend engraved bolsters with 24k-gold backgrounds.
(Mitchell D. Cohen Photography)

⌄ ANTHONY KITTEL:
Feather damascus patterning follows the lines of the 14-inch takedown bowie with she oak handle.
(Rod Hoare photo)

« JACKSON RUMBLE:
The feather damascus patterning finds its way to the tip of the ironwood-handle bowie.
(SharpByCoop photo)

» LIAM WALLE:
The blade of a 7-inch chef's knife is forged with 3,600 layers of feather damascus, and it is handled in Kauri wood with a polished bronze bolster.
(Jocelyn Frasier Photography)

« BILL RUPLE:
The back pocket folder features a Mike Tyre feather damascus blade, interior mammoth ivory handle scales, and gold pins and shield.
(Mitchell D. Cohen Photography)

» MICAH DUNN and JAMES FLEMING:
The keyhole chef's knife has a lot going on between the feather damascus blade and African blackwood handle.
(Jocelyn Frasier Photography)

» LUKE SWENSON:
The stag-handle lock-back whittler has three feathers in its caps. *(SharpByCoop photo)*

» PEYTON RAMM:
A gentleman's fighter is outfitted in a feather damascus blade and walrus ivory handle.
(Mitchell D. Cohen Photography)

« JEREMY YELLE:
A pair of chef's knives feature integral feather mosaic damascus blades and amboyna burl and Tasmanian blackwood handles.
(Jocelyn Frasier Photography)

« ELIOT MALDONADO:
To further highlight the Jim Poor feather damascus blade of a stag-handle folder, Tyler Poor engraved and gold-inlaid the bolsters in a feathery motif.
(Jocelyn Frasier photo)

« LUKE DELLMYER:
Patterning splays out from spine to edge on the low-layer feather damascus blade of a frame-handle hunter in an ironwood grip. *(SharpByCoop photo)*

« BURT FLANAGAN:
Jim Poor feather damascus makes an appearance on a traditional "Zulu" pocket folder with stag handle scales.
(Mitchell D. Cohen Photography)

» JOSH HOWARD:
Feather damascus is a fine choice for the ivory-handle trapper with a gold-inlaid shield.
(SharpByCoop photo)

» SHAYNE CARTER:
Pairing the bronze and nickel-silver guard with the walrus ivory handle was as inspired a choice as the feather damascus blade.
(SharpByCoop photo)

DUANE BOMAR:
Of the feather damascus takedown bowie ilk, mammoth ivory handle scales and floral engraving set the piece apart.
(Jocelyn Frasier Photography)

THOMAS FRANKLIN:
The feather damascus chef's knife with Koa wood handle tickles the food before it's prepared. *(SharpByCoop photo)*

BOB EARHART:
Fleshed out in feather damascus, the European red stag-handle hottie has a window pommel and a copper arrowhead overlay at the choil.
(SharpByCoop photo)

GERRY MICHAEL:
The chestnut-handle kukri is even more fly because of its feather-damascus blade.
(Jocelyn Frasier Photography)

⌃ WILLIAM BRIGHAM:
Some lucky chef brings this S-ground, feather damascus, integral beauty with amboyna burl handle to the banquet.
(SharpByCoop photo)

« TOBIN HILL:
Three Mike Tyre feather damascus blades fold out from the mammoth ivory handle of a lock-back toenail whittler.
(Jocelyn Frasier Photography)

» TREVOR MORGAN JR.:
Feather damascus splays out dramatically on an integral European chef's knife in stabilized spalted maple.
(SharpByCoop photo)

« MIKE SHINDEL:
Fighting in the featherweight class, a slim sub-hilt fighter enters the ring in a feather damascus blade, ebony handle and nickel-silver accents.
(Jocelyn Frasier Photography)

« JOHN MEDLIN: Feather damascus just feels right for the fossil walrus ivory-handle fixed blade with domed silver pins. *(SharpByCoop photo)*

⌄ HARVEY DEAN: Feather damascus patterning splays out from the centerline of a mammoth ivory-handle push dagger with gold wire inlays and gold leaf overlays. *(SharpByCoop photo)*

» JAMES INGRAM: With equal amounts feather damascus and mammoth ivory, the LinerLock folder also features an engraved stainless back spacer and titanium liners. *(Jocelyn Frasier Photography)*

« FRANK EDWARDS: A LinerLock folder parades a feather damascus blade with pure nickel shims, mammoth ivory handle scales, wrought iron bolsters, and hammered copper pins. *(Jocelyn Frasier Photography)*

« RUSSELL ROOSEVELT: This feather in the knifemaker's hat features a 1084-and-15N20 damascus blade, mild steel guard, and bone handle. *(SharpByCoop photo)*

Sculpted Steel

» FRANK EDWARDS:
There's a pearl spider in the window, a golden web, a mosaic of damascus and a completely sculpted body to boot.

(SharpByCoop photo)

« EMMANUEL ESPOSITO:
"White Fang" is a multi-ground, sculpted flipper folder featuring a marbled carbon-fiber handle frame with gold and Mokume-gane inlays.

(Mitchell D. Cohen Photography)

⌃ DAVID LISCH:
The bear head pommel of the damascus integral fixed blade is forged to shape from a pipe holding a ball bearing that "sings" when shaken.

(Jocelyn Frasier Photography)

» RICHARD ROGERS:
Sometimes, you sculpt all-steel folders in an Art Deco theme.
(Mitchell D. Cohen Photography)

» BERTIE RIETVELD:
This kaleidoscopic sculpture is executed in Dragonskin damascus and lapis lazuli, featuring a Stanhope logo. *(SharpByCoop photo)*

» JORDAN LAMOTHE:
The Kard Indian dagger features not only a "Mountain Rifle" damascus blade but also a hollow damascus handle pierced in a flower motif and a hinged butt plate that swings open to access the inside of the grip. *(SharpByCoop photo)*

» ROBERT APPLEBY:
The CPM 154 bowie is outfitted with an antique sterling silver cutlery handle sculpted to depict the ancient Roman god Janus.
(SharpByCoop photo)

» JOSE DE BRAGA:
Mother-of-pearl pushes the "Phase 2 S.E." automatic folder into warp speed.
(Mitchell D. Cohen Photography)

« RON APPLETON:
The sculpted "Azrael" dress folder is done up in the maker's Raptor-style S-7 blade, anodized 6AL-4V titanium handle, and his InfiLock mechanism. *(SharpByCoop photo)*

⩓ WOLFGANG LOERCHNER:
A fully sculpted art dagger is realized in gold, damascus and stainless steel.
(Mitchell D. Cohen Photography)

⩓ JEAN-PIERRE POTVIN:
The "Musical Knife" makes harmonious use of damascus, mammoth ivory and buffalo horn.
(SharpByCoop photo)

» WILLIAM TUCH:
The "Eclipse" dual-action auto boasts an "Odin's Eye"-pattern Damacore blade and stainless handle scales with hidden hardware to better showcase the Sergey Danilin sculpting and engraving.
(Mitchell D. Cohen Photography)

« MICHAEL WEST:
The otherworldly RWL-34-edged sculpture enlists Argentium silver and blue sunstone. *(SharpByCoop photo)*

« VINCENZO FIORE:
The integral RWL-34 Damasteel fixed blade is beautiful in its simplicity. *(SharpByCoop photo)*

Detailed Damascus

» LEE and DUSTIN PARSONS:
That gorgeous canister steel damascus blade forged from nails and 1095 deserved a black palm handle with water buffalo horn and nickel spacers. *(SharpByCoop photo)*

« ELDON TALLEY:
The Damasteel blade demands attention on the Talisong Model 3 with titanium handle halves.
(Mitchell D. Cohen Photography)

« CODY ADOLPHSON:
The Hawaiian Koa-handle bowie's "Maelstrom" damascus blade and twist-damascus guard shake things up.
(Jocelyn Frasier Photography)

» DENIS TYRELL:
You've gotta love a nice "Ocean Sunset" damascus blade (a collaboration with Rick Hall), here on an art dagger with a maple burl handle.
(SharpByCoop photo)

« EYAL LANDESMAN:
An etched and polished Damasteel "Fafnir"-pattern blade is counterbalanced by a black Timascus handle. *(Mitchell D. Cohen Photography)*

« MERT TANSU:
Few things can compete with a snakewood handle, but the seven-bar Turkish-twist damascus blade of the chef's knife does just that.
(Rod Hoare photo)

« ADAM DESROSIERS:
"Crushed Fairy Wings" damascus is the heavenly blade material for a keyhole hunter handled in stabilized curly Koa.
(SharpByCoop photo)

» BEN AKIN::
"Persian Ribbon" damascus patterning twists along the blade of a stag-handle hunter with hot-blued mild steel guard.

(Jocelyn Frasier Photography)

« BEN ABBOTT:
The horseman's axe has a detailed damascus head, a leather-over-ash handle wrapped in twisted silver wire, and brass rivets.

(SharpByCoop photo)

» JIM POOR and KELLY VERMEER-VELLA:
Jim and Kelly forged the detailed damascus blade of the "Crown Reserve Bowie" boasting a mammoth ivory handle and engraved brass guard.

(SharpByCoop photo)

STATE OF THE ART **179**

《 KEITH BARTHELMES:
"Serpent Damascus" slithers its way up to the black canvas Micarta bolster and curly Koa handle of a chef's knife.
(Jocelyn Frasier Photography)

《 D.R. DAVIS:
The large sleeveboard folder features a Mike Norris "Hornet's Nest" damascus blade and a stainless frame with integral liners and abalone inlays.
(Mitchell D. Cohen Photography)

《 CHARLIE ELLIS:
The damascus blade pattern of the petite chef's knife is based on never repeating Penrose tiling and is accompanied by a stabilized curly maple handle with G-10 chevron inlays.
(SharpByCoop photo)

》 JORDAN BUCKLEY:
A "Serpent's Tongue" damascus blade defines the ironwood-handle chef's knife with bronze guard.
(BladeGallery.com photo)

» HARVEY DEAN:
The damascus swirls like shaving cream and whiskers circling a drain. The stag razor features gold engraving and a gold escutcheon plate.
(Mitchell D. Cohen Photography)

« JOHN HORRIGAN:
At 24.25 inches overall, Turkish-twist damascus spans the greater length of the Valyrian Kings Dagger, with fluted pre-ban ivory and 18-karat twisted wire taking a position of prominence.
(Jocelyn Frasier Photography)

» GRACE HORNE:
While working away with the "Calligraphy" scissors made from Owen Bush damascus and featuring a gold pivot, pins, and rivet caps, you can always close them up for a knife in a pinch.
(SharpByCoop photo)

» DANIEL KOERT:
The way the "Huggin" Damasteel pattern spans the blade from spine to edge in layers on the "MiniSabat" folder with a titanium frame is impressive.
(Mitchell D. Cohen Photography)

» BILL BURKE:
The "Double River of Fire" damascus blade of the 8-inch chef's knife cuts the mustard while holding a curly Koa handle.
(BladeGallery.com photo)

« STANLEY BUZEK:
It's difficult to determine whether the Bill Poor "River of Fire" damascus blade, mammoth ivory handle scales or Alice Carter gold inlay and engraving are more impressive.
(SharpByCoop photo)

« DAVID LISCH:
The integral damascus fixed blade has a forged pipe handle holding a ball bearing, so the knife "sings" when shaken and is thusly named the "Singing Crusader."
(Jocelyn Frasier Photography)

« OWEN WOOD:
After forging the composite damascus blade, the maker enlisted Alice Carter to work on the gold, titanium and stainless handle.
(SharpByCoop photo)

» RON BEST:
The push dagger's dynamic damascus pattern is only equaled by the stepped handle with mother-of-pearl inlays and a diamond set in a gold bezel on the pommel.
(Mitchell D. Cohen Photography)

« DUANE BOMAR:
Check out the alternating four-bar Turkish-twist damascus blade of the 15.5-inch bowie, which has mammoth ivory handle scales and a sawblade damascus and mild steel frame.
(Jocelyn Frasier Photography)

⌄ SHAYNE CARTER:
The damascus dazzles. Paired nicely with a Koa wood handle, the hunter is a hot little number.
(SharpByCoop photo)

⌃ IAN TYSON-PICKARSKI:
A one-off, the full-tang tanto features an equally beguiling Damasteel blade, Tiffany-blue CarboQuartz bolster, and mother-of-pearl handle.
(Mitchell D. Cohen Photography)

» ANDREW MEERS:
The "Bee and Flowers Fighter" is an engraved damascus wonder in an ancient ivory grip. *(SharpByCoop photo)*

« FRANCESCO PICCININ:
The Damasteel blade of the Northern-style camp knife has a super dense twist pattern and is accompanied by a walnut handle and Karelian birch guard.
(Jocelyn Frasier Photography)

« CHARLIE LLOYD:
"Crushed W's" damascus takes centerstage on a wood-handle hunter with a 5-inch blade.
(SharpByCoop photo)

« DAVID HALL:
Reminiscent of a ship radar screen or topographical map, the 1084-and-15N20 damascus blade of the camp knife is a nice complement to the walrus ivory handle.
(Mitchell D. Cohen Photography)

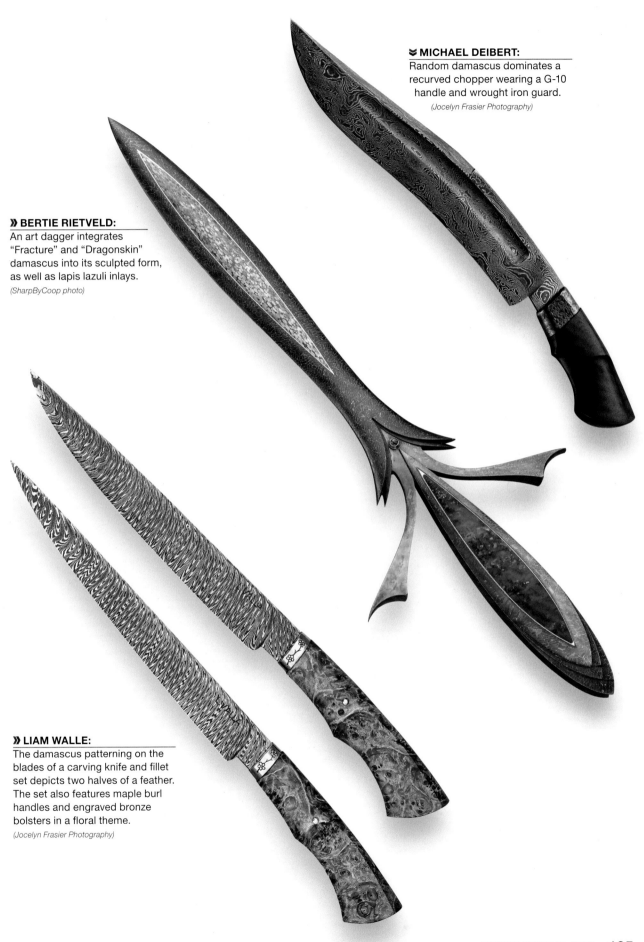

⌄ MICHAEL DEIBERT:
Random damascus dominates a recurved chopper wearing a G-10 handle and wrought iron guard.
(Jocelyn Frasier Photography)

» BERTIE RIETVELD:
An art dagger integrates "Fracture" and "Dragonskin" damascus into its sculpted form, as well as lapis lazuli inlays.
(SharpByCoop photo)

» LIAM WALLE:
The damascus patterning on the blades of a carving knife and fillet set depicts two halves of a feather. The set also features maple burl handles and engraved bronze bolsters in a floral theme.
(Jocelyn Frasier Photography)

PEYTON RAMM::
With one of the prettiest feather-damascus blades on the planet, the gentleman's bird-and-trout knife also features a walrus ivory handle and an engraved stainless guard.
(Jocelyn Frasier Photography)

JEREMY YELLE and ULYSSE ROBERT:
The bowie by Jeremy and Ulysse's folder feature matching damascus blades and mammoth ivory handles.
(SharpByCoop photo)

SIMON and JAKOB NYLUND:
Exquisite amenities of a lock-back whittler include twist-damascus blades and bolsters, checkered paper Micarta scales, and file-worked titanium liners.
(SharpByCoop photo)

LUKE SWENSON:
Three blades and a shield provided plenty of room for Chad Nichols "Intrepid" damascus to go along with the stag handle scales.
(Mitchell D. Cohen Photography)

» ZANE DVORAK:
The multi-bar damascus blade with an integral guard gets under your skin like a tapeworm, snaking around and filling all voids.
(SharpByCoop photo)

« TREVOR MORGAN JR.:
The "Crushed W's" damascus blade and integral bolster create a dizzying effect on a European-style chef's knife in an ironwood burl handle.
(Jocelyn Frasier Photography)

« JACKSON RUMBLE:
The integral dagger doesn't waste an ounce of 1084-and-15N20 damascus, sterling silver, or African blackwood.
(Mitchell D. Cohen Photography)

« DEJAN URUKALO:
The deeply etched Damasteel blade of the Sujihiki chef's knife dazzles its way to a Karelian birch handle.
(Jocelyn Frasier Photography)

⌄ ROBERT APPLEBY:
Taking sub-hilt fighter form are a 588-layer damascus blade, ladder-pattern damascus guards, and an amber sambar stag handle.
(SharpByCoop photo)

» BOBBY HOUSE:
This one's a beauty, from its "River of Fire" damascus blade to the axe handle-style European red stag handle and engraved houndstooth shield.
(SharpByCoop photo)

» PAUL PETRO:
The hunter's forged ball-bearing blade is held taut by a maple burl handle and copper Corby bolts. *(Mitchell D. Cohen Photography)*

» ERIC LUTHER:
An "Intrepid" damascus blade makes up the business end of the "Orphan" flipper folder in a titanium frame, ZircuTi bolsters and Mexican Katalox wood handle inlays.
(Mitchell D. Cohen Photography)

» HERUCUS BLOMERUS:
Tight, parallel, flattened looping lines define the Odin's Damasteel blade of the flipper folder handled in mammoth ivory.

(SharpByCoop photo)

« ERIK MCCRIGHT:
If all hunting knives had four-bar Turkish-twist damascus blades like this horn-handle beauty, no one would want to dirty them field dressing game.

(Jocelyn Frasier Photography)

« TIM ROBERTSON:
Doug Ponzio damascus pulls duty on a dazzling folder handled in bark mammoth ivory.

(SharpByCoop photo)

STATE OF THE ART **189**

« J.W. RANDALL:
An 8-inch damascus blade explodes from the stainless guard and mammoth ivory handle. *(SharpByCoop photo)*

» STEPHAN FOWLER:
A hunter and bowie/fighter showcase matching Tiger damascus blades and guards and ancient ivory handles. *(SharpByCoop photo)*

« BRIAN BROWN:
A large finger hole pierces the Damasteel blade of the "Mini Yeager" featuring textured bolsters. *(Mitchell D. Cohen Photography)*

» MATT HUMPHRIES:
The maker was so ecstatic when he saw the Jim Poor damascus blade he engraved the entire frame of a lock-back folder, inlaying it with mammoth ivory, gold and fine silver. *(SharpByCoop photo)*

» CHAD KIMMELL:
The aptly named "Main Vein" chef's knife incorporates a CruForgeV and 15N20 "Flipped Feather Crushed W's" damascus blade, a Koa wood handle, and a box elder burl frame.

(Jocelyn Frasier Photography)

« CHARLES COOK:
The big old cedar-handle whopper chopper comes with a 160-layer 1095-and-15N20-damascus blade that won't quit.

(SharpByCoop photo)

» JIM POLING:
Damascus patterning is used to maximum effect, from edge to spine, on the 2-inch convex-ground blade of a small walnut-handle model.

(SharpByCoop photo)

» RYAN SCHWARTZ:
Even a small blade is good for showing off Bertie Rietveld damascus, accompanied here by a Fatcarbon "Space Coral" carbon-fiber grip.

(Mitchell D. Cohen Photography)

» JORDAN LAMOTHE:
The "Deep Roots" damascus chef's knife branches out into a sculpted curly acacia handle with ebony and stainless inlays.
(SharpByCoop photo)

⌄ BARRY BARNARDT:
The "Little Dragon" front flipper shows off its Bertie Rietveld "Dragonskin" damascus blade and snakewood handle.
(BladeGallery.com photo)

« BUBBA CROUCH:
Let's hear it for "Herring" damascus, and two blades' worth via a double trapper with stainless bolsters and integral liners, a Remington jigged-bone handle, and Troy Flaharty engraving.
(SharpByCoop photo)

Carved to Perfection

» FRANCK SOUVILLE:
Daggers, flowers, and a skull, scorpion and squawking bird are carved by Serge Raoux into the mammoth ivory grip of a damascus folder.

(SharpByCoop photo)

» BROCK WOODSON:
The chef's knife is a beauty from its copper damascus san mai blade with copper shims to its carved blister maple handle.

(Jocelyn Frasier Photography)

« LARRY FUEGEN:
Of sole authorship, the damascus lock-back folder features a fully carved mother-of-pearl handle, sculpted bolsters, and gold pins and bail.

(Mitchell D. Cohen Photography)

» JORDAN LAMOTHE:
The rare damascus hunting knife
in a fluted desert ironwood handle,
the fittings are blued steel with silver
and gold koftgari (Indian damascene work
in which steel is inlaid with gold) in a morning
glory motif. *(SharpByCoop photo)*

« FRANK EDWARDS:
Carved mother-of-pearl handle scales,
file-worked liners and sculpted
bolsters highlight a damascus
LinerLock folder.
(Jocelyn Frasier Photography)

» PAUL DISTEFANO:
The ivory Micarta handle of a
mosaic damascus hunter is carved
with Japanese maple leaves and
birds native to the country.
(Jocelyn Frasier Photography)

» GEORGE GAO:
The Damasteel of a gent's interframe folder envelops an ox bone handle inlay carved in a feather motif.

(Rod Hoare photo)

« FERNANDO NUNES:
The Mediterranean dirk is engraved by Luis Gil and features an antique ivory handle carved to bloomin' perfection.

(SharpByCoop photo)

« SHANE TAYLOR:
A carved ebony handle, engraved spine and textured bronze bolster are just some of the amenities of the "Batwing Kukri" in an incredible two-bar damascus blade. *(Jocelyn Frasier Photography)*

Sans Straight Lines

So many knifemakers talk about curves, and not just regarding pretty ladies, but also the lines of cars, boats, motorcycles, sculptures, and, of course, knives. They often relate knives to sportscars, talking about smooth transitions, airflow, handling, aerodynamics, and sexy features like their favorite vehicles' fins, scoops and fenders. The artists inside them come out when they see a sports car.

Straight lines don't seem to have the same effect, and random curvy lines don't quite measure up. It's the sexy curves, smooth, flowing lines and subtle bumps that do it.

Knives without straight lines often feel better in the hand and are easier to grip, wrap one's fingers around and choke up on. They follow the curve of the leg, the palm of the hand, or the bulge of a hip. They ride along seamlessly in sheaths or clipped to pockets, and they handle, well, like sportscars.

There's something appealing about bends and curves. And while there's plenty of room for straight edges, utility knives, sheepsfoot blades and Wharncliffe models, it's the knives sans straight lines that are heating up the highway and revving makers' engines.

《 CLAUDIO and ARIEL SOBRAL—CAS KNIVES: It doesn't get curvier than the "Snake," featuring a hand-forged san mai blade with sweeping grinds and a sculpted and contoured carbon-fiber handle. *(BladeGallery.com photo)*

《 BERTIE RIETVELD: She's a curvy "Flirt" dressed in a Nebula blade, zirconium guard and handle and fine silver inlays. Her maker added his signature Stanhope logo. *(SharpByCoop photo)*

« MICHAEL HOBBS:
Birch burl and damascus bend in all the right places on a recurved, tapered-tang fixed blade. *(SharpByCoop photo)*

⌃ KRYSTLE MARTINEZ AULTMAN:
The sans-straight-lines push dagger is developed in Alabama Damascus and mammoth ivory and delivered in a buffalo hide sheath.

⌃ TASHI BHARUCHA:
The hollow-ground, recurved CPM 154 blade of the flipper folder is as clean and curvaceous as the titanium frame, and zirconium backspacer and pivot collar.
(SharpByCoop photo)

» SETH LOPEZ:
The very definition of a keyhole dagger suggests no straight lines, as exemplified here in damascus and African blackwood.
(SharpByCoop photo)

Meteoric Makeup

For as long as man has been gazing at the sky (and that's a long time), people have been fascinated with space, stars, the moon, sun, planets and other celestial bodies. So, how cool is it when a meteoroid, which is usually a fragment from a comet or asteroid, comes barreling down to earth, where it lands with a thud unnoticed for days, weeks, months, years or decades until someone stumbles upon it or stubs a toe walking?

They say meteors typically become visible about 62 miles above sea level. There are also meteor showers, in which no meteor lands on Earth but passes by in streaks of light. An estimated 25 million meteoroids enter Earth's atmosphere each day.

A meteorite is the remains of a meteoroid that has survived entrance into the Earth's atmosphere and hit the ground. So, what could be more otherworldly than a knife handle, bolster, guard or even a blade made from meteorite? Any bladesmith worth their salt can tell you how dense and hard alloys become through heat and movement, and meteorites are no different. They also pick up character in their travels through space, like Neil Armstrong or Buzz Aldrin.

The meteoric makeup of today's high-tech knives is The Right Stuff.

« NATE "TUNA" GRANT:
The magical blade forged from a meteorite and 1095 keeps the company of brass and cocobolo.
(SharpByCoop photo)

« KIRK MAYBERRY:
The "Stubby Rhino" showcases a "rhino hide frame" with meteorite inlays and backspacer.
(Mitchell D. Cohen Photography)

《 JACO DE KOCK:
Gibeon meteorite is set on polished titanium liners for the handle of an "SL Flipper" with a stainless Damasteel blade, titanium pivot, and heat-colored titanium-damascus pivot collar. *(BladeGallery.com photo)*

》 ADAM PARKER:
The aptly named "Space Rocks" small bowie boasts a meteorite canister damascus blade, brass guard, and ringed Gidgee handle. *(Rod Hoare photo)*

》 RUBEM LORENZ:
Bob Loveless-style drop-point hunters have mammoth ivory handles and meteorites planted in the bolsters.
(SharpByCoop photo)

Maestros of Mosaic Damascus

These artistic masters work in the steel medium, making alloys come alive in intricate patterns. Their methods vary. Some forge traditional steels, stacking them first, then folding and cutting, restacking, folding, and reforging many times before finally flattening the billets, finishing and etching. Others prefer powdered metals, canisters, square dies, or tubes. They, too, forge the blades, but only after the patterns have been predetermined in their steel encasements. The forge takes patience and time, work and determination.

The maestros of mosaic damascus have been known to push and pull patterns with handheld hammers, using the forges as their friends, shaping billets until patterns flow with the edges of the blades. Some have attempted serpentine multi-bar patterns, blades with integral mosaic bolsters or extremely high numbers of forge welds for complex mosaic damascus blades.

Do they whistle while they work or blast Beethoven on the radio while they perform their steel ballet? Visit their shops to find out, or stare into the steely blades, letting the music the maestros have created envelop the senses and tell you a story.

« FRANCESCO PICCININ: The hunter's 5.5-inch twisted mosaic damascus blade was forged by Fucina Fogonero to accompany a hornbeam handle and carbon-fiber guard.
(Jocelyn Frasier Photography)

« FRANK EDWARDS: Gold inlay and engraving span the mosaic damascus handle and blade of a folding dagger with black-lip pearl handle inlays.
(SharpByCoop photo)

» DE WET VAN ZYL:
A multi-bar composite mosaic damascus blade clears the way for a camp knife hafted in curly maple and given a polished brass guard.

(BladeGallery.com photo)

« COLTON ARIAS:
The blade, guard, pommel nut and pommel of the takedown quillon dagger are mosaic damascus, and the double-edged beauty has a leather- and wire-wrapped handle.)

(Jocelyn Frasier Photography)

« MIKE QUESENBERRY:
Mosaic damascus, pearl and gold have starring roles on an integral dagger that fully disassembles.

(SharpByCoop photo)

« SHANE TAYLOR:
Dragon damascus breathes its fiery character across the blade of a LinerLock folder in mammoth ivory handle scales.

(Jocelyn Frasier Photography)

» RONNIE SMITH:
Make way for the mosaic damascus fighter in a blued guard, copper spacer and fossilized walrus ivory grip.
(Mitchell D. Cohen Photography)

» MATT MCGUIGAN:
The maker describes the mosaic damascus blade of the "Eagle Ray Bowie" as resembling a school of spotted eagle rays.
(Jocelyn Frasier Photography)

» WILL STELTER:
The integral Gyuto chef's knife is all about the movement of the mosaic damascus blade and amboyna burl handle.
(SharpByCoop photo)

≪ KEITH BARTHELMES:
A new favorite blade steel might be "Electric Flower" mosaic damascus, here on a gentleman's cleaver with a polished, octagonal G-10 handle.
(Jocelyn Frasier Photography)

≫ JACKSON RUMBLE:
The true treats of a 15-inch bowie are the mosaic damascus blade and ringed Gidgee handle.

(SharpByCoop photo)

≫ RIAN DOUDLE:
An antler-handle bowie is the beneficiary of a mesmerizing 6.25-inch mosaic damascus blade. *(Rod Hoare photo)*

≰ PAUL DISTEFANO:
While a mother-of-pearl cherry blossom and jade frog embellish the African blackwood handle on one end, a mosaic damascus blade holds its own on the other.

(Jocelyn Frasier Photography)

« BRAD QUILL:
Mosaic damascus and "Pale Moon" ebony make for a perfect pairing on a flat-ground takedown bowie. *(Rod Hoare photo)*

» TREVOR MORGAN JR.:
The 15.5-inch fighter features a maple burl handle and an explosive recurved "Explosion" mosaic damascus blade.
(Jocelyn Frasier Photography)

» JACCO VAN DE BRUINHORST:
Only a crosscut mammoth ivory handle and clamshell guard could have competed with the 10.5-inch mosaic damascus blade of a takedown bowie.
(SharpByCoop photo)

» ALEX HOSSOM:
Though the patterning is reminiscent of the form, the mosaic damascus kitchen knife with maple burl handle is no snowflake.
(Mitchell D. Cohen photography)

« SCOTT GALLAGHER:
The folder features a mosaic damascus blade with 14k-gold Dellana dots, dinosaur bone handle inlays, and a stainless frame. *(Jocelyn Frasier Photography)*

» WILLIAM BRIGHAM:
The maker's integral mosaic damascus includes patterns that morph into new designs before one's eyes, all anchored by a pretty piece of palpable amboyna burl. *(SharpByCoop photo)*

» JACOB GAETZ:
Many a hunter would benefit from a mosaic damascus and redwood burl model like this. *(Jocelyn Frasier Photography)*

» DAVID LISCH:
The marvelous mosaic damascus blade is guarded by pure iron covered with melted gold and anchored by a gold-wire-wrapped fluted blackwood handle. There's also a gold-covered finial and domed gold spacer to appreciate. *(SharpByCoop photo)*

≪ JESSE HU:
Mosaic damascus hits the mark on a 10.5-inch bowie, boasting a ringed Gidgee handle and stainless guard. *(Jocelyn Frasier Photography)*

» RYAN SEARLS:
Parts of a takedown fighter include a mosaic damascus blade with a 15N20 core and a 24k gold-plated edge, a carved mammoth ivory handle, mother-of-pearl underlay, and a mild steel guard and pommel featuring 18-karat gold melted onto their surfaces.

(Jocelyn Frasier Photography)

⌃ KELLY VERMEER-VELLA:
While the spider damascus captures you in its web, the fluted black-lip pearl handle, twisted gold wire, Tyler Poor engraving, and diamond in the thumb stud will make you yearn for freedom (and money).

(SharpByCoop photo)

⌃ JOHN H. DAVIS:
Mosaic flame damascus sets the folder on fire, contrasting with the white mother-of-pearl handle and blued titanium liners.

(SharpByCoop photo)

STEVE SCHWARZER:
Maestro Steve Schwarzer forges a mosaic canister damascus blade for the "Shark Knife" and lets it and the fossil walrus ivory tail do the talking.
(Jocelyn Frasier Photography)

MATT PARKINSON:
The Ashokan Moon mosaic damascus blade shows the maestro at the peak of his career.
(SharpByCoop photo)

ANTHONY STOVALL:
If the Robert Eggerling mosaic damascus blade of the stag-handle hunter with bronze guard and butt cap doesn't get your juices flowing, you might be comatose.
(Jocelyn Frasier Photography)

JEREMY YELLE:
The bowie lets its "Jellyroll Mosaic Twist Damascus" blade splay out, anchoring the edge with a stag body.
(Jocelyn Frasier Photography)

ANDREW BLOMFIELD:
Stars alight on the mosaic damascus blade of a sub-hilt fighter with an ironwood handle, leaving trails to the edge and spine.
(SharpByCoop photo)

Still Life Scrimshaw

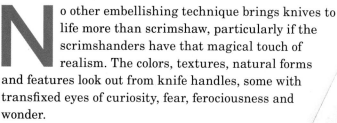

No other embellishing technique brings knives to life more than scrimshaw, particularly if the scrimshanders have that magical touch of realism. The colors, textures, natural forms and features look out from knife handles, some with transfixed eyes of curiosity, fear, ferociousness and wonder.

Knifemakers hire scrimshaw artists to turn edged tools into functional art. Proper pictures are painted using needles, engraving tools, inks, and dyes, with the colors pricked beneath the surfaces of ivory, faux ivory, bone and horn, giving the figures depth and deep color saturation.

Artists of this level project beautiful images onto stable surfaces meant to be held and admired. They specialize in still-life scrimshaw and turn knives into living beings.

≪ DR. TERRY SCHREINER:
This fly fishing companion comes dressed in a Damasteel blade, Jerry McClure titanium damascus bolsters, anodized titanium liners, gold thumb studs, and mammoth ivory handle scales scrimshawed by Alice Carter.
(SharpByCoop photo)

⯆ HERUCUS BLOMERUS:
There's nothing sheepish about the big horn scrimshaw by Carina Meyer on the Westinghouse Micarta handle of an M390 flipper.
(SharpByCoop photo)

» TOM PLOPPERT:
The cowboy saddle-horn folder rides in Rick Dunkerley mosaic damascus blades, mammoth ivory handle scales scrimshawed in a cattle drive motif by Raluka Markon, and Paul Markon-engraved bolsters.
(Mitchell D. Cohen Photography)

» DENNIS FRIEDLY:
While Linda Karst Stone scrimshawed the fossil ivory handle of the damascus dagger in a jungle's worth of colors, Alice Carter gold inlaid and engraved the guard and ferrule. *(SharpByCoop photo)*

« MANUELE MESSORI:
Pearl inlays extend from the blade to the handle, where Luca Roccaforte scrimshaws them in scary-good human (or android?) faces.
(SharpByCoop photo)

Struck by the San Mai Smiths

Imagine the discipline, commitment and endurance it took to forge the first san mai blade in the 14th century, one with a hard hagane edge born from iron sand. The sand was placed in a tatara (clay furnace), heated to 1,000 degrees Celsius (1,800-plus degrees Fahrenheit), and mixed with charcoal to add carbon to the steel. We're talking 36–72 hours—a day and a half to three days—of adding sand every 10 minutes before breaking the clay tub and removing the steel. The best steel was on the edges of the resulting metal block, where oxidation was stronger. The bright silver pieces were ideal for blades.

But not just any blades—the hagane was only part of the process of forging tamahagane steel, which has soft outer layers that give the blades flexibility without breaking.

Some knifemakers still smelt steel from iron sand, but not many. And while the process is refined and easier using modern equipment, much remains the same. Smiths still have it in them to forge san mai blades, finishing and etching the steel to show the hamons, or temper lines, that indicate a transition from hard edge to softer outer layers. It's in their blood. The steel struck by san mai smiths embodies discipline, commitment and endurance.

« JOHN ARNOLD:: The maker forged SG2 san mai damascus for the coffin-handle front flipper folder in "Silver Strike" carbon-fiber scales.
(BladeGallery.com photo)

« BUBBA CROUCH: The Bakers Forge "Copper Mai" blade is a little vein of riches for the trapper with copper pins and shield and an antique Micarta handle.
(SharpByCoop photo)

BRIAN EFROS:
"Sonic Doom" faces the apocalypse in a Chad Nichols random-pattern Armorcore damascus blade, black and white synthetic bone handle and black Timascus pocket clip.
(Mitchell D. Cohen Photography)

PAT BIGGIN:
A black ebony-handle bowie features a stunningly beautiful san mai blade and a guard of 1700s colonial wrought iron from the Boston Harbor. *(Jocelyn Frasier Photography)*

JAKE SUMMERELL:
Standouts of a Gyuto chef's knife includes a Takefu Vtoku-2 clad damascus blade, a blackwood bolster and a spalted tamarind handle.
(Rod Hoare photo)

MICHAEL ANDERSSON:
As any good Swedish knifemaker would, Andersson equips his san mai damascus bowie with a clamshell guard and engraved reindeer antler handle.
(BladeGallery.com photo)

《 DAVE ARMOUR:
The san mai steel sends shockwaves up and down the blade of the hunter in a copper guard and stabilized maple burl handle.
(SharpByCoop photo)

》 ERIC LUTHER:
The Baker Forge CuMai blade of the "Orphan" model with a frag-patterned titanium frame is incredible. *(Mitchell D. Cohen Photography)*

》 KELLY FRASIER:
A "GoMai" blade gets things going alright on a hunky fighter with a curly mango handle and wrought iron guard.
(Jocelyn Frasier Photography)

》 RIAAN MANSER:
An SG2 san mai damacus blade is accompanied by a keyhole-style faux ivory handle on the "W5 Midi Flipper."
(BladeGallery.com photo)

⌃ DENIS TYRELL:
More than 2 ounces of gold are forged into the san mai damascus blade of a chef's knife handled in maple burl. *(SharpByCoop photo)*

⌃ BRIAN BROWN:
The strikingly beautiful "Custom 51" tanto folder blends a Mike Norris san mai blade with a titanium frame.
(Mitchell D. Cohen photography)

⌃ SHANE ATWOOD:
Copper damascus with a 1084 core is the piping hot blade material of a desert ironwood-handle hunter featuring a woolly mammoth tusk bolster.
(Jocelyn Frasier Photography)

» TOM BULLOCK:
The "Hephaestus" CuMai slip joint folder is worthy of its Greek god namesake (of blacksmiths nonetheless), here in a paper Micarta handle.
(BladeGallery.com photo)

« MILAN POKORNY:
"The Swan" struts its Futuron Forge CPM 154-core damascus blade, titanium-zirconium guard, and carbon-fiber handle with mosaic mother-of-pearl inlays.
(SharpByCoop photo)

» ALEX HOSSOM:
Despite the singular san mai blade, gorgeous cottonwood handle, and Richlite bolster, the "Revenge 2" fighter remains stealthy.
(Mitchell D. Cohen Photography)

⌃ JORDAN BUCKLEY:
The 15N20-and-copper CuMai blade of the hunter includes a 1084 core and is offset by a blue-dyed and stabilized curly mango handle.
(BladeGallery.com photo)

⌃ BROCK WOODSON:
The atypical camp knife comes in a san mai damascus blade with copper shims, a 3,200-layer core, a Koa handle, and a brass guard.
(Jocelyn Frasier Photography)

≪ WILLIAM "COREY" REYNOLDS:
The clad damascus and copper GoMai sawback blade of the bowie butts up against a bronze guard and woolly mammoth tooth handle.
(SharpByCoop photo)

⌃ JIM PROVOST:
The "Tiger GoMai" blade in a raindrop pattern wears its stripes well on a 3.5-inch drop-point hunter handled in Koa wood. Dirk Loots engraved the guard.
(Jocelyn Frasier Photography)

⌃ RICHARD COOPER:
Dressed in a 100-layer damascus blade clad with an Apex Ultra core, the chef's knife also features a purple acacia wood handle and G-10 and stainless spacers. *(Rod Hoare photo)*

⌃ DE WET VAN ZYL:
The hand-forged san mai blade with a 52100 core should do the trick for a chef's knife in a dyed and stabilized maple handle and brass bolster.
(BladeGallery.com photo)

≫ MARK SMITH:
The damascus and copper Go Mai blade is as bitingly beautiful as the mokume-gane guard and masur birch handle of the bowie.
(SharpByCoop photo)

» FRANCOIS MAZIERES: The clad damascus and 15N20 GoMai blade of the paring knife was forged in collaboration with Peter Cocks and complemented by resonated wine stopper spacers and a stabilized ringed Gidgee handle. *(Rod Hoare photo)*

» CLYDE CHALLENOR: The "Viper RT" front flipper sports a Damacore san mai blade forged by Damasteel, a titanium handle frame, and black Timascus inlays. *(BladeGallery.com photo)*

« CHARLES CARPENTER: Classic bowie styling includes a san mai blade, damascus, stainless steel and bronze guard, and a desert ironwood handle. *(SharpByCoop photo)*

« GREGORY CIMMS: The CuMai blade of the "Tuna Sword" was forged by the maker to accompany a bronze guard and curly Narra and bog oak handle. *(SharpByCoop photo)*

» CLARENCE DEYONG: With two layers of copper, the clad blade has a 1094 core and is accompanied by a black cherry burl handle. *(Mitchell D. Cohen Photography)*

» CHRIS CROMBIE:
The recurved 1084 san mai bowie boasts nickel shims, a black G-10 guard, and a Bocote wood handle.

(Rod Hoare photo)

» PEDRO GONZALEZ:
Working in concert together on a 9-inch chef's knife are a raindrop pattern Schichi-Mai damascus blade by Baker Forge and Tool, a carbon-fiber handle, woolly mammoth tusk bolster, and black and red G-10 liners.

(Jocelyn Frasier Photography)

« BILL OGDEN:
All three blades of the little "Pusher" models are from the same bar of Robert Eggerling san mai steel and feature white paper Micarta, heat-blued damascus and stabilized moose horn handles.

(SharpByCoop photo)

Daggers to the Heart

« JIM SORNBERGER:
The San Francisco dagger showcases an ATS-34 stainless blade, a gold quartz and lapis lazuli handle, and full engraving by the maker. *(SharpByCoop photo)*

« JON MOORE:
Random-pattern damascus, giraffe bone and brass only seem like odd bedfellows until one sees the resulting dagger.

« A. BRETT SCHALLER:
The maker's Zero-G CPM 154 daggers come in a choice of Timascus, dyed maple burl, and imitation ivory handles.
(SharpByCoop photo)

« GRANT and GAVIN HAWK:
The "Deadlock C" (top) out-the-front dagger is a collaboration with Serge Knives, while the Deadlock B below it is Grant and Gavin's carbon-fiber handle model.
(Mitchell D. Cohen Photography)

⌄ JOT SINGH KHALSA:
Beaded silver wire wends its way around the fossil walrus ivory handle of a stainless damascus dagger with carved sterling guard.
(SharpByCoop photo)

⌄ BRAD MILLMAN:
The dagger is decked out in a three-bar twisted W's damascus blade, a maple burl handle, and textured and forged stainless and copper fittings.
(Jocelyn Frasier Photography)

» CHUCK IANNI:
Fluted curly maple is a classy choice for the grip of a damascus dagger.
(Mitchell D. Cohen Photography)

⌄ NEELS VAN DEN BERG:
Perhaps foreshadowing a future use, the "Shattered Glass" damascus ring dagger sports a bronze guard and a fluted, silver wire-wrapped mammoth tusk handle. *(SharpByCoop photo)*

« VLADIMIR KOLENKO: Hallmarks of an art dagger include Bertie Rietveld "Dragonskin" damascus, sterling silver, gold, lapis lazuli, and garnets. *(SharpByCoop photo)*

⌃ FRANK EDWARDS: If looking for an automatic folding dagger, one would be wise to choose the feather damascus model in white mother-of-pearl and 24-karat gold. *(Jocelyn Frasier Photography)*

⌃ SETH LOPEZ: This one dazzles in 1080-and-15N20 damascus, African blackwood and 24-karat gold leaf. *(SharpByCoop photo)*

» JERRY HOSSOM: The "Apex Proto" in a CTS-XHP blade and black Micarta handle points the way. *(Mitchell D. Cohen Photography)*

⌃ ANDREW MEERS: A wide, leaf-shaped mosaic damascus blade of the "Lion's Dagger" is like a mane on the jungle king. *(SharpByCoop photo)*

» JEAN-PIERRE POTVIN:
Done up in twist damascus, brass and black ebony, it's a complete package in or out of the sheath. *(SharpByCoop photo)*

» WOLFGANG LOERCHNER:
A hand-sculpted dagger is dressed in stainless steel, damascus and gold.

(Mitchell D. Cohen Photography)

» JIM POLING:
Let the rosewood-handle dagger with a 5160 blade and mild steel guard into your heart.

(SharpByCoop photo)

» JACKSON RUMBLE:
The mammoth ivory handle is fluted and wire wrapped while the damascus blade has a deep, tapering fuller.

(SharpByCoop photo)

⌃ VINCE EVANS:
It's a pattern-welded ear dagger with a blackwood handle, bronze guard, engraving and a pommel that resembles an ear, but I wouldn't stick it there.

(SharpByCoop photo)

« GREG GOTTSCHALK:
Mokume-gane and damascus share billing on a frame-handle dagger with file-worked guard.
(Mitchell D. Cohen Photography)

⌃ BOB EARHART:
The Spartan Dagger, complete with hammered copper spartan helmet overlays on the pommel, sports a 300-layer damascus blade and a silver wire-wrapped, fluted Gaboon ebony handle.
(SharpByCoop photo)

⌃ DANIELE IBBA and LANA GORSKA:
When you've got Bertie Rietveld "Dragonskin" damascus like that, you fashion a sculpted dagger with a lapis lazuli handle, Fabio Bregoli engraving, and a "golden cage" pommel set with blue diamonds and housing a lapis lazuli ball. *(SharpByCoop photo)*

» JERRY HOSSOM:
The fantastic "Morgul Blade" is a damask, iron and brass creation.
(Mitchell D. Cohen Photography)

⌃ JASON KNIGHT:
The "Knight" dagger does battle in 80CrV2 steel, wrought iron and wenge wood.
(SharpByCoop photo)

» TOM OVEREYNDER:
Dressed in "Dragonskin" damascus and a carbon fiber handle, the "Galactic Traveler" boasts four colors of gold dot inlays, and Brian Hochstrat blued fittings. *(SharpByCoop photo)*

⌃ HARVEY DEAN:
Of sole authorship, the mammoth ivory-handle, gold-inlaid and engraved damascus dagger is a looker. *(SharpByCoop photo)*

⌃ BERTIE RIETVELD:
As if the maker's "Dragonskin" damascus weren't enough, the "Lady Luck" dagger also showcases a gold-inlaid colored stainless handle and a removable magnetic pommel through which to view a stanhope lens. *(SharpByCoop photo)*

» PETER JOHNSSON:
Eos, the goddess of dawn and dusk, inspired the glint of silver and gold and the shades of the blackened iron on the hilt of the sword, which also features a damascus blade and leather grip studded with sterling silver pins. *(SharpByCoop photo)*

» ANDREW BLOMFIELD:
The gold inlaid, engraved, fluted and wire-wrapped handle of a feather damascus dagger is enough to get the juices flowing. *(SharpByCoop photo).*

« MATT PARKINSON:
With a slightly fluted, carved handle and silver guard, the dagger is a delightful rendition. *(SharpByCoop photo)*

« ROBERT APPLEBY:
Moose antler provides a solid grip for the Michael Price-style ring dagger in a hollow-ground CPM 154 blade. *(SharpByCoop photo)*

« JOHN HORRIGAN:
A fluted-handle model is made up of Turkish-twist damascus, case-hardened 1040 steel, African blackwood, and twisted 18k-gold wire. *(SharpByCoop photo)*

» JOSEPH BANDEKO:
A double-keyhole dagger is done up in a 15N20 blade with a super fuller, an African blackwood handle and a stainless pommel. *(SharpByCoop photo)*

« HAROLD PARSONS:
The tightly patterned Turkish-twist damascus blade is impressive enough, let alone an ironwood handle and nickel-silver guard and pommel. *(Jocelyn Frasier Photography)*

Engraved & Enlivened Steel

» DENNIS FRIEDLY:
To celebrate 50 years of knifemaking, Gil Rudolph was commissioned for some golden engraving, and Tanner McFall and Robert Eggerling, respectively, to provide the damascus for the blade and guard of the maker's anniversary fighter.
(SharpByCoop photo)

« DANIEL KEOWN:
The trapper with colorful rag Micarta handle is engraved by Lisa Tomline in an enchanted rose theme for a friend celebrating his wife's surviving breast cancer.
(Mitchell D. Cohen Photography)

« RICK EATON:
The mosaic damascus "Dragon Slayer" sidelock folder with gold-lip-pearl scales is engraved in arabesque banknote with a Celtic knot bordering the pearl. A dragon attacks a knight on one side of the handle, and on the other side, the knight is shown on a horse after killing the dragon. *(Francesco Pachi Photography)*

« MANUELE MESSORI:
Engraved in a dragon and undead Samurai theme, the "Little Blue" frame-lock folder has a Damasteel blade and Fat Carbon "White Storm" zirconium frame. (SharpByCoop photo)
(Rod Hoare photo)

« AUDRA DRAPER:
An all-integral damascus chef's knife is embellished with fleur-de-lis engraving and an engraved silver plate.
(Jocelyn Frasier Photography)

» MAL HANNAN:
The stainless fittings and blade of a stag-handle dagger proved the perfect palette for Phil Vinnicombe engraving.
(Rod Hoare photo)

« MIKE SMITH:
Pearl and Damasteel would have been impressive enough, but the Dale Bass gold-inlay and engraving take the folders to a whole new level.
(SharpByCoop photo)

» ANTONIO FOGARIZZU:
A dagger of gold and black-lip pearl is engraved by Manrico Torcoli in a nude warrior princess theme.
(SharpByCoop photo)

⌄ GLENN WATERS:
A gorgeously engraved double-action auto folder is further embellished by Shibu Ich Gin (silver and copper) bolsters, Russian mammoth ivory handle scales, 24k-gold inlays, and a topaz on the button release.
(Mitchell D. Cohen Photography)

⌄ MAMORU SHIGENO:
The Bob Loveless-style City Knife showcases an ATS-34 blade, stag handle scales, and Naoya Ishikawa engraving.
(SharpByCoop photo)

⌃ CHRIS HAMELIN:
Wolfgang Loerchner engraved the copper bolster of the Saratoga Hunter, dressed here in black G-10, copper, and a 440C blade.
(Jocelyn Frasier Photography)

》RICK DUNKERLEY:
Gold inlay and engraving highlight a small Persian folder in feather damascus and carved black-lip pearl. *(Mitchell D. Cohen Photography)*

》ELIOT MALDONADO:
As wavy lines of Damaworks stainless damascus enliven the blade, scrolls engraved by Tyler Poor envelop the blue bolster screw of a mammoth ivory-handle fixed blade. *(SharpByCoop photo)*

《JIM POOR:
The "Fancy Bull Cutter" dress locking folder sports a damascus blade dripping with character and a gorgeous grip engraved by Tyler Poor. *(SharpByCoop photo)*

《BOB MERZ:
The Wes Griffin engraving on the auto button and bolsters is inspired and a nice touch on the CTS-XHP folder handled in mammoth ivory. *(SharpByCoop photo)*

» TIM HERMAN:
The engraved and gold-inlaid folder with black-lip mother-of-pearl inserts is of sole authorship.
(Mitchell D. Cohen Photography)

« BERTIE RIETVELD:
With a Dumortierite stone handle, "Dragonskin" damascus blade, and Jonathan Knoesen engraving, the "Royale" dagger lives up to its name.
(SharpByCoop photo)

» GRANT and GAVIN HAWK:
An out-the-front "Deadlock Model C" dagger is fabulously engraved by Wilfred "Chip" Valtakis II of Chipped Metal.
(Mitchell D. Cohen Photography)

« CASEY BERRYHILL:
Bolster engraving by Alice Carter is a nice transition from the Damasteel blade of the dogleg folder to the mammoth ivory handle.
(SharpByCoop photo)

» TONY BAKER:
Even the gold handle inlay is engraved on the large auto dagger that features a 416 stainless frame fully embellished in a scroll and floral motif by Alice Carter and a Damasteel "Hakkapella" blade with 14-karat rose gold pins.
(SharpByCoop photo)

⌄ HAROLD PARSONS:
Amenities of an 11.5-inch 1095 dagger include a giraffe bone handle with black G-10 liners and some stylistic engraving on the nickel-silver guard.
(Jocelyn Frasier Photography)

» STEVE LINDSAY:
Only diamonds and precious metals were good enough to honor the Golden Retriever immortalized on the bolster of a Frank Lindsay art folder.
(SharpByCoop photo)

« EDMUND DAVIDSON:
Scroll and leaf engraving by Wendy Crowell nearly spans the length and width of the integral cleaver/chopper with a Siberian mastodon ivory handle. *(SharpByCoop photo)*

⍥ BRIAN MILINSKI:
A stainless damascus blade meets a fossilized mammoth tusk handle at a stainless bolster engraved by Tyler Poor. *(Jocelyn Frasier Photography)*

⍥ JOHNNY STOUT:
Bolsters engraved and gold-inlaid by Dale Bass take their place between a Jim Poor feather-damascus blade and mammoth ivory handle scales. *(SharpByCoop photo)*

» TOM OVEREYNDER:
"Cowboy up" with the two-blade, jigged-handle folder engraved by Alice Carter. *(SharpByCoop photo)*

» TOM PLOPPERT:
An Arkansas lock-back hunter set showcases CPM 154 blades and springs, cape buffalo horn and bark mammoth ivory handle scales and Tim George engraving.
(Mitchell D. Cohen Photography)

» HERUCUS BLOMERUS:
The full-scale engraved ZircuTi handle of the flipper folder, complete with silver inlay, garners attention.
(SharpByCoop photo)

⌃ OWEN WOOD:
Art Deco engraving by Ron Skaggs enlivens a damascus folder.
(Mitchell D. Cohen Photography)

⌃ BUBBA CROUCH:
Tasteful touches of gold inlay and engraving, courtesy of Alice Carter, span the CPM 154 trapper with stag handle scales.
(SharpByCoop photo)

» REINHARD TSCHAGER:
Engraved by Italian master Valerio Peli, the RWL-34 fixed blade exhibits a mammoth ivory handle, gold inlay, and a gold chain and fob.
(Mitchell D. Cohen Photography)

⌃ MATT HUMPHREYS:
Success could be defined as making and carrying an engraved sterling silver and gold trapper with CPM 154 blades. *(SharpByCoop photo)*

❧ FRANK CENTOFANTE:
Built by the late, great maker, the pearl-handle tail-lock folder is respectfully engraved by Simone Fezzardi in a samurai and dragon theme.

(SharpByCoop photo)

❧ FABRIZIO SILVESTRELLI:
The clean RWL-34 blade and fossil mammoth ivory handle allow the Valerio Peli gold inlay engraving to shine.

(SharpByCoop photo)

» DAVID BROADWELL:
A handle of bronze and titanium is treated to Ray Cover Jr. gold inlay and engraving, accompanied by a Bill Poor feather damascus dagger blade and sculpted bronze guard.

(SharpByCoop photo)

⌃ ROBERT CHAMPION:
The aptly named Lonestar leaves it all out there in Jimmy Floyd carbon damascus, titanium, mammoth ivory and Dale Bass gold inlay and engraving.

(SharpByCoop photo)

» KELLY VERMEER-VELLA: The "finer things in knife" include a san mai blade of 1084 steel, spider damascus and 22-karat gold, a handle of black-lip pearl, 24-karat gold and mild steel engraved by Tyler Poor, and a diamond set in the thumb stud. *(SharpByCoop photo)*

⌄ JIM SORNBERGER: Engraving in a Neptune with a trident sea theme exquisitely covers the silver sheath of an ATS-34 art knife in 14-karat gold and gold quartz. *(SharpByCoop photo)*

» FRANCOIS DU TOIT: The titanium handle of the Damacore TF-4 Folder is gold inlaid and engraved in a dragon theme by one Armin Winkler. *(SharpByCoop photo)*

⌃ STANLEY BUZEK: A gent's knife with a bold Bill Poor "River of Fire" damascus blade, the star of the show is the puzzle-like Alice Carter handle engraving with gold ribbon running throughout. *(SharpByCoop photo)*

FACTORY TRENDS

As Steve Shackleford noted in the September 2023 issue of *BLADE* Magazine, no single knife company won more than one Knife-Of-The-Year® Award at the '23 BLADE Show. The fact that there were 13 awards and 13 winners indicates the competition among the world's best factory knife companies is hotter than ever. In fact, three companies won their first-ever Knife-Of-The-Year Awards: Shirogorov Knives, Rosecraft Blades and GiantMouse, winner of the Overall Knife of the Year®.

So, what's driving the competition? The knife market is strong, driven by innovation, engineering, state-of-the-art steels and materials, and demand and need for quality edged tools and weapons. Crossover markets' increasing knife demand includes guns, the military, hunting, fishing, outdoors, camping, bushcraft, cooking, kitchen, restaurant, and food service. Television and reality shows have brought knives to a larger market, as have successful trade shows such as the BLADE Show, BLADE Show West and BLADE Show Texas. Cutting competitions have amassed followers, and survival series have attracted a rapt audience of enthusiasts.

Knife companies collaborating with custom knifemakers on designs and manufacturing have elevated production knives to new levels, which is evident in the newest blades on the market today, from machetes and everyday carry knives to flipper folders, replaceable blade folders, pocket machetes, cleavers and modern hunters. Production knife offerings cover the needs of today's enthusiasts who demand higher quality at lower prices.

Knife customers seek out high-tech steels, natural and synthetic handle materials, innovative locks, complete sheath systems, smooth pivots, and countless ways to open, close, access, and conceal their blades of choice. They want carry, color, steel and material options, and ways to take apart and assemble their knives. This is the new knife reality—the Factory Trends of knives—and there are more options than ever.

FROM PENNY KNIVES TO POCKET FOLDERS

Gain a better appreciation of the hobby via a trip through pocketknife history.

Feature and photos by David W. Jung

In 1991, hikers climbing in the mountains between Austria and Italy discovered a frozen body that they believed was recently deceased. They had discovered the 5,000-year-old body of Ötzi, the Iceman, not only well preserved but with all his tools and supplies in excellent condition. Along with his clothes, food, and hunting gear, Ötzi also had a knife, sheath, and pouch that could be tied to his waist. Ötzi's pouch was meant for carrying small items. Thousands of years later, someone came up with the idea of sewing such pouches to clothing, thus inventing pockets.

Ötzi carried a small fixed-blade flint knife, which was the standard cutting tool for thousands of years. Through the evolution of craftsmanship came folding knives for the few who could afford them. With the economy of scale provided by the Industrial Revolu-

tion, prices began to fall, the pocketknife became affordable to the general population, and the fixed blade was relegated as a tool for the outdoors rather than everyday carry. By looking at the historical rise of the pocketknife, we can better understand the cutting tool we depend on daily.

Knives that once cost an exorbitant amount could later be had for a few pennies. By examining the past, we can better understand the present and appreciate the rich history of our hobby.

The Roman Empire extended into Britain and as far north as present-day Germany, known then as Germania. Some of the earliest pocketknives were carried by Romans and employed for the same things we use them for now. If we look at an example of a Roman pocketknife, we first notice a well-preserved bronze handle in contrast to a badly corroded iron

The Benchmade Immunity is an example of a small knife with outsized capability. Like the Roman folding knife, it has a metal handle, though anodized aluminum rather than bronze, and its CPM-M4 blade is light years ahead of an ancient iron blade in performance.

Early examples of the Chinese fish knife were found in Xian, China. They represent a traditional working knife design for peasant fishermen. Even though the knives were basic and prone to rust, they provided an inexpensive tool to cut the line and mend fish nets.

blade. This bronze versus iron condition contrast is typical in museum collections worldwide. In archeology, bronze has excellent staying power, while ancient iron blades are rarely discovered without extensive rust.

The Roman-Germania knife could be considered a gentleman's or lady's knife. It would have been more expensive than a fixed blade and potentially a symbol of wealth. Because of the cast-bronze handle and the need to engineer a pivot, manufacture would have been limited to skilled craftsmen, and most surviving examples are in museums.

Many ancient Roman knives were figural, meaning the bronze handles had been cast in the shapes of animals or people. Perhaps they would be treated like an amulet or represented a favorite animal. Without blade-locking systems, friction folders were best suited for light use. The small blades could have been useful when eating, as Romans did not have widespread access to forks. Fixed blades were used for defense and aggressive cutting.

The "Lost Roman Knife" replica designed by Condor Knives accurately represents a Roman fixed-blade tool used for everyday carry and resembles many edged tools in European museums.

The Penknife

With time, the small folding gentleman's knife found many uses, one for the educated class as a penknife. These small knives were primarily employed to sharpen pen nibs and points for writing. A beautiful example is the knife given to George Washington by his mother when he made his way in the world as a young man. As seen in the replica made by Schrade, the blade is delicate with ornate mother-of-pearl scales. Wealth meant education and power, and this type of knife wasn't available to the public until the Industrial Revolution. Providing mother-of-pearl handles came at a high cost to the workers who finished them, as the dust was toxic, and many suffered from repeated exposure.

Today, with ballpoint pens, pencil sharpeners, and cell phones, the gentleman's knife is more likely to be used for hobby needs and everyday cutting. One modern interpretation is the Benchmade Immunity. Designed in-house, it has the advantage of high-end

Since our ancestors lacked pockets, tools were carried in pouches or rolled up in animal skins. Larger tools could be crafted at the site of an animal kill, while others were part of the hunter's traveling gear. The first tools were knapped or fractured rocks. Wood and bone were also shaped for scrapping skins and mild cutting.

The Spyderco Native 5 Salt sports a MagnaCut blade, represents a modern take on a knife designed for saltwater sports and trades and provides a high level of cutting performance.

Left: Gentlemen's knives come in many shapes and sizes, most with blades on the shorter side of the spectrum. The clear-handle Ontario Wraith, popular Chris Reeve Sebenza, Spyderco Chaparral, Al Mar Denali (ahead of its time in the 1990s), and WE Baby Banter represent modern takes on gentlemen's knives. The Scrimshawed Parker, Abalone Shell Inlay Hiro, Schrade George Washington Pen Knife replica, and Schrade Lady Leg are elegant versions of past knives.

Below: The earliest examples of penny knives had simple, round wood handles and inexpensive iron or steel blades. Later examples, like the German-South African Okapi, French Opinel, and German Mercator, added locks, while the Spanish Pallares knife was a slip joint. The Japanese Higonokami trusts friction and thumb pressure on the blade tab to secure the blade when open.

steel technology along with a proven blade lock. The Immunity folder boasts a 2.5-inch, Cerakote-finished CPM-M4 blade hardened to 62-64 RC on the Rockwell Hardness Scale, a coated aluminum handle, and cutting performance outpacing its ancestors. With a nominal three-finger handle, it's up to the lanyard and dangler bead to give the little finger something to grip for blade control. The coated blade has a shallow edge curve, and the acute point is ideal for piercing. The knife is a good example of maximum performance in a compact size.

Benchmade consciously decided to design a petite gentleman's folder for specific areas where knife blade length is restricted, such as in some government buildings. Real gentlemen like to carry knives, even at work in an office building.

The Spyderco Chaparral Lightweight with a 2.79-inch CTS-XHP blade and gray fiberglass-reinforced-nylon handle scales is an ideal compact gentleman's knife in the same ilk as the perennial favorite Chris Reeve Small Sebenza with titanium frame-lock. Some of the smaller models from Buck Knives, Civivi, Gerber, Kershaw, Spyderco, CRKT and SOG also fall into this category. It all comes down to your everyday needs and the depth of your wallet.

The penny knife was a small pattern available to the masses with the rise of commercial workshops and factory production. These inexpensive knives filled a need for everyday carry by the common man. Some early versions include the wooden penny knife with a thin blade dating back to the 1400s in Europe. With a round lathe-turned wood handle and a simple triangular iron or steel blade, the knife was inexpensive to produce and remained popular into the 1700s. Later, French knives, such as Opinel production folders with wood handles and simple blade designs, continued the penny knife tradition.

With time, the turned wood handles gave way to horn and stag scales, and external spring locks became common. Some companies produced inexpensive stamped metal handle knives like Germany's famous Mercator Kat Knife. Another German company manufactured the simple external back-lock Okapi knife series, which was later produced in South Africa and is said to have skinned more animals in Africa than any other knife.

Rapid industrialization in Europe drove the popularity of penny knives. Cities in larger European countries were centers for knife production. These included Albacete, Spain; Theirs in France; Solingen, Germany; Maniago in Italy; and Sheffield, England. Many of the same countries also had centers dedicated to swords and armaments, but they weren't necessarily located in the same city.

American Knife Production

In America, knife production spanned several Eastern states. Production numbers followed the rise of industrialization, and knife designs paralleled those of Europe. Each side of the ocean would attempt to overshadow the other with industrial production. An interesting fact about the rise in popularity of the American bowie knife is that thousands of "Official Bowie Knives" were crafted in Europe to fill the high demand stateside. Europe continues to be a supplier of knives to this day, but in much smaller numbers after U.S. production climbed with the expansion of industrial centers.

In Japan, the penny knife was represented by the Higonokami. This simple 1800s friction-lock design was carried in the pockets of the Japanese until the 1960s. The government banned almost all knives after a political assassination occurred on live TV, with the assailant using a samurai sword. Until then, boys would carry Higonokami knives to sharpen

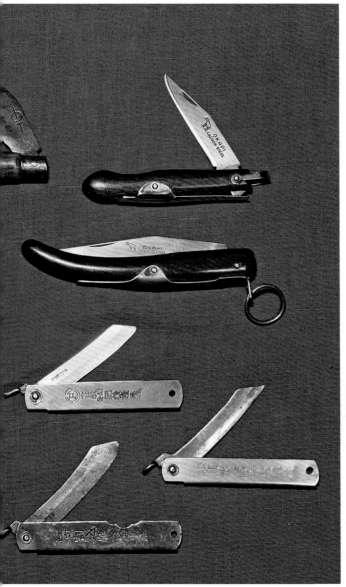

One doesn't associate ancient Rome with pocketknives, but early examples like the one at the bottom can sometimes be found in Roman ruins. Restricted to the wealthier citizens of the Roman Empire, it's easy to see the knife DNA that continues today. For most Romans, the knife of necessity would be very similar to the Condor Brand "Lost Roman" fixed blade at the top.

The Benchmade Weekender combines two premium Diamond Like Coated (DLC) CPM S90V stainless steel blades and a bottle-cap lifter in a traditional camper design. The CPM S90V steel is significantly harder than a traditional camper's knife. With durable Burgundy Micarta handle scales allowing for a good grip, the end user can enjoy a premium knife in a classic design.

their pencils and make wooden and bamboo toys. The Higonokami name was trademarked to the guild of knifemakers in the Higo (now Kumamoto) Prefecture in Japan. At one time, 40 workshops were making them. Today, one workshop remains; the knives are tourist items rather than practical tools.

The penny knife still exists in spirit, if not in name. Internal back springs sandwiched between handle halves eventually replaced the early external spring locks. This streamlined the handle design and facilitated snag-free pocket carry. Companies like Opinel and Okapi still make the original design, and all major knife companies endeavor to have an entry-level model that can be purchased at big box stores for reasonable prices. Unfortunately, there are also cheap knock-off knives of dubious quality and unknown steels flooding the basement of the market

to be sold at gas stations and swap meets, so buyers beware.

If one type were associated with the outdoors, it would have to be the camper's knife, the Boy Scout Knife, the Scout Knife, the U.S. Military Utility Knife, or even a generic boy's pocketknife or jackknife. With the typical implement array including a blade and three additional tools, the camper's knife became associated with the scouting movement where it was recognized as the perfect tool for camping.

The mass-produced camper's knife originated in the 1900s as a less expensive version of a late-1700s to 1800s German or Swiss folding hunter or soldier's knife. The Official Scout Knife, which included two versions, was introduced in 1911 in America. With its success, the floodgates were open for millions of similar models.

The military also needed a deployment utility knife, and contracts were awarded to both sides of the Atlantic. In Europe, the Germans dominated the market, with the Swiss Army Knife a response to the Germans cornering the market. The same companies that made Scout knives also manufactured military versions in America. At first, they were of the same construction as Scout knives, but that changed during World War II when a transition was made to stainless handle scales instead of wood, bone, or stag.

With military contracts for millions of knives during the war, many found their way back to the States via returning servicemen. After the war, production continued at a reduced but steady pace. Post-war Europe saw an influx of American occupational troops, and again, many servicemen returned home carrying the distinctive red camper-type Swiss Army Knives made by Victorinox or Wenger.

The versatility of the multiple blade and tool combinations made the classic camper's knife special. Even the military versions had models for different branches and specialties such as electri-

If there is a knife style that says pocketknife, it would have to be the Scout/Camper/Utility knife of the 20th century. Regardless of the name, this basic multi-blade design was produced in the millions for camping and war. Though originating in Europe, America adopted the knife for everyday and outdoor use, and its popularity is only now being challenged by the versatile multi-tool.

cian, medic, Marines, and Army. These knives remain popular, with Victorinox/Wenger of Switzerland producing an astonishing 45,000 daily.

Modern Camper's Knife

Bringing the idea of a camper's knife into the world of high-tech blade steel, the Benchmade Weekender provides a glimpse of what can be achieved when production quality outclasses inexpensive mass production. With two Diamond Like Coated (DLC) CPM-S90V stainless blades reaching 59–61 RC and a bottle-cap lifter, the Weekender blades are significantly harder than the typical camper's knife. The addition of burgundy Micarta scales also allows for a durable handle. While this high-tech knife costs more than some traditional models still available, the end user can now enjoy the highest performance options in a classic design.

While the camp knife has been immensely popular over the years, a threat emerged to its success. That competitor is the multi-tool popularized by Leatherman of Portland, Oregon. Where campers or soldiers once carried a multi-blade knife, they now carry a multi-tool and often an additional single-blade knife that can be opened quickly.

Another early folder, the fish knife, was likely discovered in a flea market in Xian, China. Xian was the terminus of the Silk Road, which allowed the transfer of goods between China and the Central Europe and Middle East regions. Aptly named, the folding knife is shaped like a fish, features a marlin spike "tail," and the blade only pivots halfway open. A safe assumption is that the primary use of a fish knife was to repair fishing nets. The theory is that the blade only opened halfway to prevent using it as a weapon, but that's not well documented. The circa-1800s knife is not a high-end tool, but a Chinese fisherman used what he could afford. Rust was an issue for the knives, a problem for fishermen today.

However, the situation is far better for the modern sportsman or anyone who works around water. MagnaCut, one of the latest steel alloys, comes from the mind of Larrin Thomas. With a family history in knifemaking and a doctorate in metallurgical engineering, Thomas formulated MagnaCut to be an outstanding knife steel with excellent corrosion resistance. Spyderco employs MagnaCut blades on the company's Salt series of knives designed for saltwater exposure. The U.S.-made Spyderco Native 5 Salt represents a modern take on a knife designed for saltwater sports and trades, complete with cutting performance.

Unlike the primitive Chinese fish knife, the bright yellow Native 5 Salt has a serrated edge. Serrations gained popularity in the 1950s and '60s with the rise of frozen foods and the poor performance of early stainless steel. When cutting fibrous material like rope, the serrated edge is advantageous for fishermen, divers, dockworkers, soldiers, sailors, and rescue crews.

As knife enthusiasts, we are fortunate. If there was ever a golden age of knives, this is it. Never in history have we had as many options for affordable, quality knives, high-performance, state-of-the-art masterpieces and everything in between. When the buyer sticks with reputable brands and companies that are honest about what they're selling, it is difficult to go wrong.

Previously, quality folding knives were restricted to a few wealthy individuals. Today, enthusiasts can find many acceptable knives at various price points. For knife enthusiasts, there are thousands of affordable vintage collectibles and many great new blades, from penny knives to pocket folders. □

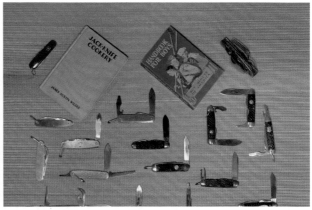

Thousands of affordable scout, military and camp knives are available to collectors and enthusiasts.

MEATY MACHETES

Some mighty meaty machetes include, from top to bottom, the Gerber Gator Bolo, ESEE Knives Expat Darien Machete, Schrade Decimate Bolo and TOPS Knives Yacara 10.0. *(Marty Stanfield photo)*

REPLACEABLE BLADE PARADE

Perfect for the pocket or toolbox, the replaceable blade knives, from left to right, are a Hogue Expel Scalpel 2.5, Coast 1919 Reserve Shift, Havalon Piranta Bolt, and Kershaw LoneRock RBK2. *(Abe Elias photo)*

EDC AND FLIPPER FOLDERS

» From Top to Bottom on Each Page: Modern everyday carry (EDC) and flipper folders are coming out of the woodwork (and knife-works of America.) They include the GiantMouse GMX EDC folder, Buck Knives 590 Paradigm damascus flipper, Maserin W1 EDC, Kershaw Iridium EDC, WE Knife Solid flipper, and Shirogorov Knives Mini Quantum CD flipper.

BELLYFUL BLADES

⌃ Bellying up with big blade bellies are, from top to bottom, the Condor Black Leaf folder, TOPS Field Dog, Benchmade S45VN Taggedout, and V Nives ADAPPT. *(Marty Stanfield photo)*

Three of the latest factory-assisted opening folders are, from left to right, the Kershaw Flyby, Bear Ops Swipe A100-AIBK-S, and SOG Flash AT.
(Marty Stanfield photo)

FOLDING POCKET CLEAVERS

⌃ Ideal for everyday carry, folding cleavers are trending in the knife industry and include, from top to bottom, the Smith's Titania Cleaver, SOG Stout FLK Cleaver, and Kershaw Strata Cleaver. *(Marty Stanfield photo)*

KNIFEMAKERS INDEX

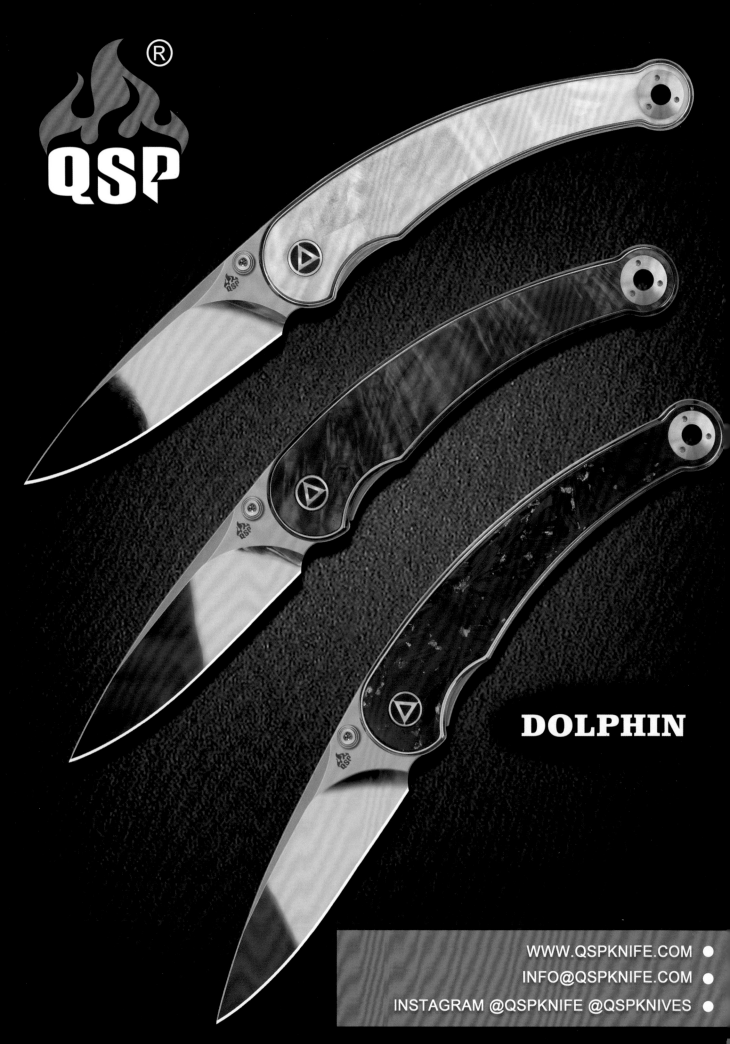

QSP®

DOLPHIN

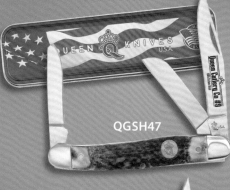

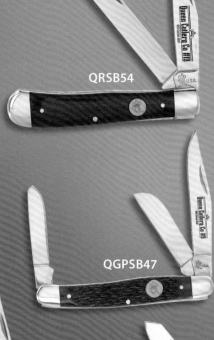

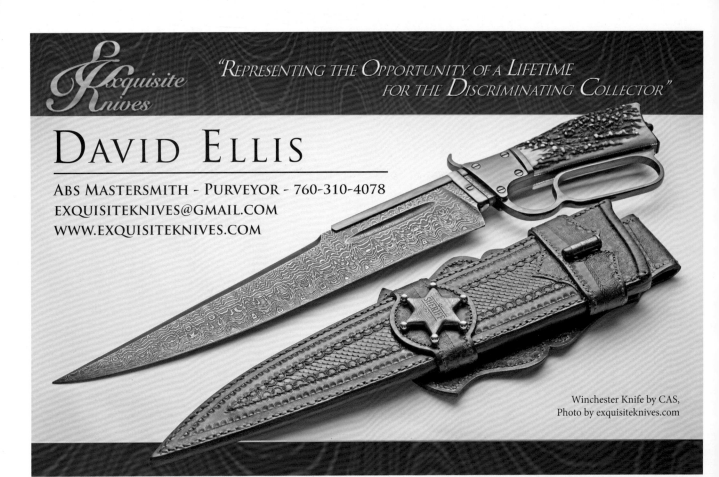

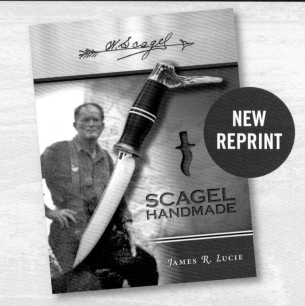
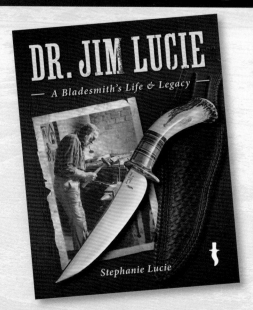

FARINA FINE ARTS

Wilderness with
Westinghouse Micarta
By R.W. Bob Loveless

Photography
by Mitchell D. Cohen

www.farinafinearts.com
studio@farinafinearts.com
+1 617-470-8862

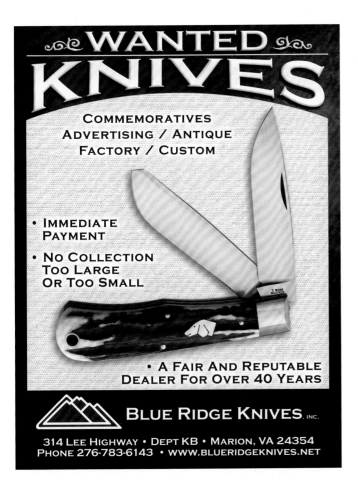

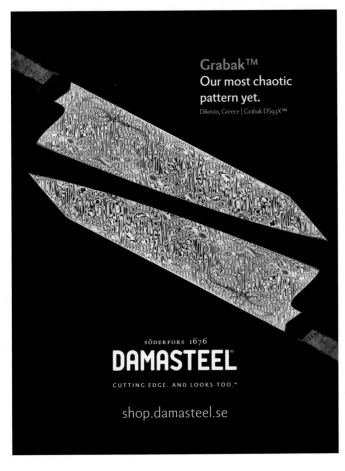

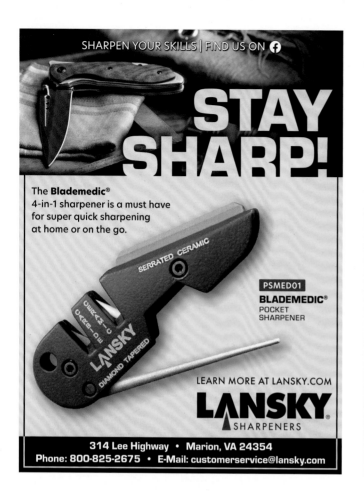
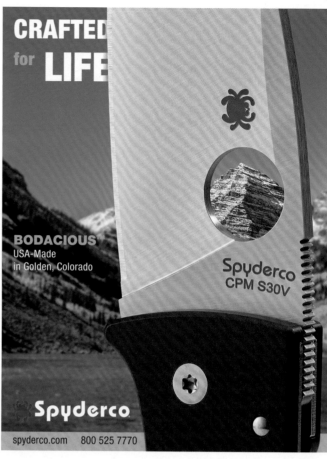

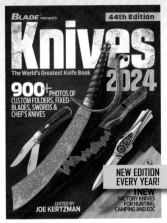
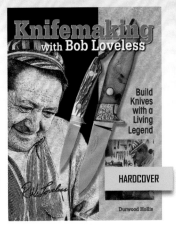

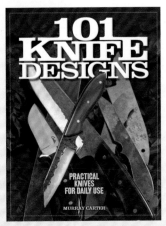
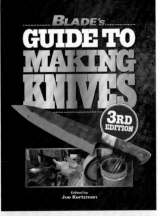

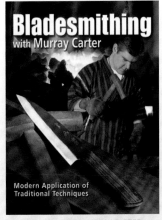

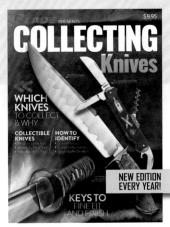

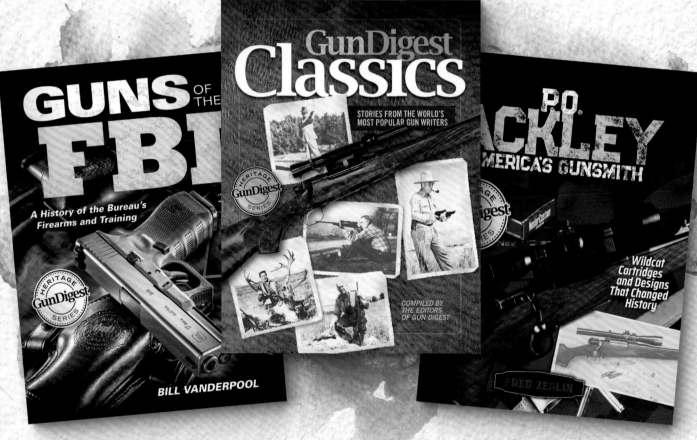

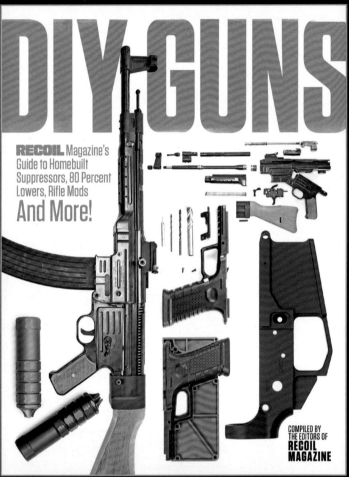
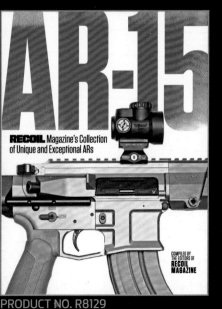